St

D0424699

In This Book

QuickStart Guide

Your keys to understanding the cities – we help you decide what to do and how to do it

Need to Know
Tips for a smooth trip

Neighbourhoods
What's where

Explore Bilbao & San Sebastián

The best things to see and do, neighbourhood by neighbourhood

Top Sights
Make the most of your visit

Local Life
The insider's city

The Best of Bilbao & San Sebastián

The cities' highlights in handy lists to help you plan

Best Walks
See the city on foot

Bilbao & San Sebastián's Best...
The best experiences

Survival Guide

Tips and tricks for a seamless, hassle-free city experience

Getting Around
Travel like a local

Essential Information
Including where to stay

Our selection of the cities' best places to eat, drink and experience:

◉ **Sights**

✖ **Eating**

🍷 **Drinking**

✦ **Entertainment**

🔒 **Shopping**

These symbols give you the vital information for each listing:

📞 Telephone Numbers	👪 Family-Friendly
🕐 Opening Hours	🐾 Pet-Friendly
🅿 Parking	🚌 Bus
🚭 Nonsmoking	⛴ Ferry
@ Internet Access	Ⓜ Metro
📶 Wi-Fi Access	Ⓢ Subway
🥗 Vegetarian Selection	🚊 Tram
📖 English-Language Menu	🚆 Train

Find each listing quickly on maps for each neighbourhood:

Bar Hemingway

16 🍷 Map p233, B2

Legend has it that Hemi
self, wielding a machine
erate this timber-pan
ered bar during
showpiece is a
en by Papa ar
town. Dress
s.com; Hôtel Rit
. 🕐6.30pm-2a

16 🍷

6 ◉ *Plac
Va*

Lonely Planet's Bilbao & San Sebastián

Lonely Planet Pocket Guides are designed to get you straight to the heart of the city.

Inside you'll find all the must-see sights, plus tips to make your visit to Bilbao and San Sebastián really memorable. We've split the cities into easy-to-navigate neighbourhoods and provided clear maps so you'll find your way around with ease. Our expert authors have searched out the best of each city: walks, food, nightlife and shopping, to name a few. Because you want to explore, our 'Local Life' pages will take you to some of the most exciting areas to experience the real Bilbao and San Sebastián.

And of course you'll find all the practical tips you need for a smooth trip: itineraries for short visits, how to get around, and how much to tip the guy who serves you a drink at the end of a long day's exploration.

It's your guarantee of a really great experience.

Our Promise

You can trust our travel information because Lonely Planet authors visit the places we write about, each and every edition. We never accept freebies for positive coverage, so you can rely on us to tell it like it is.

The Best of Bilbao & San Sebastián 119

Survival Guide 137

QuickStart Guide

Welcome to Bilbao & San Sebastián

Alike but not alike, Bilbao and San Sebastián are both cities with a Basque soul and a love of the culinary arts. But where Bilbao is industrious and arty, San Sebastián is flirty and sunny. And in between the two? A string of bijou coastal villages with a sea-salt heart.

San Sebastián
PEETER VIISIMAA/GETTY IMAGES ©

Bilbao & San Sebastián
Top Sights

Museo Guggenheim Bilbao (p36)

A byword for contemporary architecture, Bilbao's spectacular Museo Guggenheim has lifted the city into the 21st century and changed the face of regional tourism.

Museo de Bellas Artes (p40)

From Gothic sculptures to pop art, the Museo de Bellas Artes is the region's most compelling collection of fine art. Temporary exhibitions draw huge crowds. Above: *Garden*, by Francisco Iturrino

San Sebastián Aquarium (p74)

More than just pulsating jellyfish, gardens of coral and an awful lot of fish, San Sebastián's aquarium also features a captivating Basque whaling exhibit.

Playa de la Concha (p88)

Fulfilling almost every expectation of what a perfect city beach should be like, San Sebastián's Playa de la Concha is among the best in Europe.

San Telmo Museoa (p72)

San Sebastián's showpiece cultural attraction is this impressive museum of Basque culture and society. Exhibits can be challenging, but they are always interesting.

Monte Igueldo
(p90)

Take a clunky old-world funicular railway to the summit of Monte Igueldo for eagle-eye views of San Sebastián; finish with a few turns on the carousel.

Central Basque Coast (p66)

Where the storm-tossed Atlantic Ocean is fighting a duel with the green hills and plunging valleys. The result is a contorted and spectacular coastline, dotted with lovely fishing villages.

Guernica (p64)

It doesn't always make for pleasant viewing, but Guernica's peace museum will get you thinking about war, hate, discrimination and love.

Bilbao & San Sebastián Local Life

Insider tips to help you find the real city

Once you've ticked off the obligatory sights, you can experience the region as the locals do by exploring one of these walking and *pintxo*-tasting routes through the Basque Country's best.

Bar-Hopping in Bilbao (p32)

▶ *Pintxos*
▶ Nightlife

Come early evening, each and every bar in Bilbao turns into its own little carnival of chatter, music and exceptionally good food. Don't miss the *pintxo*-bar lined Plaza Nueva, which hosts a flea market on Sunday mornings.

Following the Pintxos Trail (p76)

▶ *Pintxos*
▶ Nightlife

San Sebastián is one of the world's great foody destinations and holds more Michelin stars per capita than any other city in the world. But its real culinary star is the *pintxo* (Basque tapas). The locals like nothing better than wandering from bar to bar, sampling one *pintxo* after another.

STEFANO POLITI MARKOVINA/JAI/CORBIS ©

Classic Spanish octopus *pintxos* (tapas)

Café Iruña (p50)

Other great places to experience the cities like a local:

Parque Natural de Urkiola (p26)

Parque Natural de Gorbeia (p44)

Riverside Walks (p98)

Sagüés Sunsets (p105)

Café Iruña (p50)

Punta Galea (p61)

Playa de Hondarribia (p114)

Duesto (p52)

Bilbao & San Sebastián
Day Planner

Day One

Start in Bilbao with breakfast in the Moorish-like surroundings of **Café Iruña** (p50). Afterwards, follow the river up to the **Museo Guggenheim Bilbao** (p36) remembering to allow plenty of time to admire the mesmerising exterior of the iconic building and the sculptures, fountains and river views that surround it. For lunch get your first taste of gourmet Basque cooking in Michelin-starred **Nerua** (p48), the Guggenheim's stylish restaurant. Book ahead in busy periods.

In the afternoon walk through the dreamy **Parque de Doña Casilda de Iturrizar** (p44) and then head to the **Museo de Bellas Artes** (p40) whose permanent collection of fine art says to the Guggenheim that it's what's on the inside that counts. If time allows head to the **Euskal Museoa** (p25) for a Basque history lesson.

In the evening stroll the busy, narrow old town streets grazing on *pintxos* (tapas) in any one of dozens of bars. The **Plaza Nueva** (p33) is a particular culinary hot spot and there is often a buzzing atmosphere here on weekend nights. If the night is still young, head to **Kafe Antzokia** (p52) for some alternative Basque culture.

Day Two

Rather than taking the motorway direct to San Sebastián, take some time to explore the area around Bilbao and its battered coastline. The undulating road makes for a slow, spectacular drive with dramatic seascapes at every turn and cute fishing towns nestled in every sheltered nook. Start off in Getxo, home to a popular beach and the Unesco-listed **Puente Colgante** (p58), before heading eastwards to Guernica. This, the site of a terrible wartime atrocity and inspiration for one of the world's most famous artworks, boasts a moving **museum** (p65).

In the afternoon drive past the pretty towns of Mundaka and Elantxobe, pausing in gorgeous **Lekeitio** (p68). On a hot summer day you'll certainly want to build sandcastles on one of its beaches.

As the day cools down drive into San Sebastián and head straight for the world-renowned *pintxos* bars of the old city. We love **La Cuchara de San Telmo** (p77), but you can hardly go wrong in any bar here.

Short on time?
We've arranged Bilbao and San Sebastián's must-sees into these day-by-day itineraries to make sure you see the very best of the city in the time you have available.

Day Three

☀ San Sebastián is a city geared to the finer things in life – this is a day to relish. Start with a little morning culture in the challenging **San Telmo Museoa** (p72), which showcases Basque identity through a sometimes loosely knit, but always fascinating, set of exhibitions. If that's not for you, check out the living exhibits in the city's stellar **aquarium** (p74). Afterwards climb to the summit of nearby **Monte Urgull** (p79) for memorable panoramas.

☀ For lunch you're spoilt for choice: sample some slap-up fried fish by the harbour or legendary *pintxos* in the old town. With the day heating up, it's time to worship the sun on one of San Sebastián's near-perfect beaches. Head to **Playa de la Concha** (p88) for glitz or **Playa de Gros** (p105) for surf.

☽ For dinner, dress smart (and book way ahead) for a meal you'll never forget at Michelin-starred **Arzak** (p134), one of the best restaurants on the planet.

Day Four

☀ Although San Sebastián hogs all the attention, venture out of town and you'll find there's plenty of interest on the coast, as well as some superb seafood to be eaten. Kick off in Pasajes, a short bus ride from town – it's even better as a memorable three-hour hike. Here you can learn about the area's whaling history at the **Albaola Foundation** (p113) and visit Victor Hugo's one-time holiday home, now the **Casa Museo Victor Hugo** (p113). Lunch at **Casa Cámara** (p115).

☀ Next, push on to Hondarribia, the last Spanish town before the French border. Explore the hilltop **Casco Histórico** (p113) and the **Iglesia de Santa María de la Asunción** (p114), a striking architectural hybrid. Then, for a complete change of scene, check out the seafront promenade and, if the weather's up to it, head for a swim at the sheltered **beach** (p114).

☽ Spend the evening on **Calle San Pedro** (p114), Hondarribia's most beautiful and lively street with its classic *pintxo* bars and popular restaurants. Top eating choices include **Gran Sol** (p117) and **Ardoka** (p117).

Need to Know

**For more information,
see Survival Guide (p137)**

Currency
Euro (€)

Language
Spanish (Castilian) and Basque

Visas
Generally not required for stays of up to 90 days. Some nationalities need a Schengen visa; EU/Schengen residents need no visa at all.

Money
ATMs widely available. Credit cards accepted in most hotels, restaurants and shops.

Mobile Phones
Local SIM cards widely available and can be used in most unlocked GSM phones. Data coverage is good in cities and towns.

Time
Western European (GMT/UTC plus one hour during winter, plus two hours during daylight savings).

Plugs & Adaptors
Plugs have two round pins; electrical current is 220V/230V.

Tipping
Small change (€1 per person in restaurants) and rounding up (in taxis) is usually sufficient.

Before You Go

Your Daily Budget

Budget less than €80
▶ Dorm beds €15–20; *hostal* (budget hotel) doubles €50–70
▶ Three-course *menú del día* lunches €10–12
▶ Plan sightseeing around free admission

Midrange €80–200
▶ Double room in midrange hotel €75–150
▶ Lunch and/or dinner in decent restaurants €15–20
▶ Use discount cards to keep costs down

Top End more than €200
▶ Double room in top-end hotel from €150
▶ Fine dining for lunch and dinner €30–180

Useful Websites

Basque Country (www.basquecountry -tourism.com) Regional tourist office site.

Bilbao Turismo (www.bilbaoturismo.net) Bilbao tourist office site.

San Sebastián Turismo (www.sansebastian turismo.com) San Sebastián tourist office site.

Lonely Planet (www.lonelyplanet.com) Destination information, bookings, traveller forum and more.

Advance Planning

Three months before Book a room in San Sebastián, up to six months ahead between Easter and October.

Two months before Book a table to remember at Arzak.

One week before Book online tickets for the Guggenheim to avoid queues.

2 Arriving in Bilbao & San Sebastián

Most people arrive in the Basque Country by air. Three airports serve this region: Bilbao, San Sebastián and Biarritz. Because the San Sebastián airport is domestic and has limited flights, many San Sebastián–bound visitors actually fly into nearby Biarritz in France. Frequent buses link all these cities, and airports, with one another.

✈ From Bilbao Airport

▶ Buses run every 20 to 30 minutes to central Bilbao (€1.40, 20 minutes), stopping at Plaza de Federico Moyúa and Termibus (the bus station).

▶ Taxis from the airport to the city centre cost €23 to €26.

▶ Buses to San Sebastián (€15.70, 1¼ hours) run hourly.

✈ From San Sebastián Airport

▶ Bus E21 runs hourly to San Sebastián (€2.35, 30 minutes), stopping at Plaza de Gipuzkoa.

▶ Buses to/from Biarritz airport (France; €4.55, one hour) run seven times daily.

✈ At the Airports

Bilbao, San Sebastián and Biarritz airports are small but well organised. In Bilbao and Biarritz, domestic and international flights share the same terminal. There are ATMs, cafes, car parks and car hire at all airports.

3 Getting Around

Both Bilbao and San Sebastián are small cities and very pedestrian friendly. From the point of view of a visitor, the easiest way to get around either city is usually on foot. However, Bilbao does have an excellent tram, metro and bus system that is worth using if you want to get from one end of the city to the other. San Sebastián has a city bus network, but travellers rarely need to use it.

M Metro

There are two Bilbao metro lines which meet at Sarriko. The most useful stations for tourists are Moyúa, Abando and Casco Viejo. Trains run every few minutes from 6am until 11pm. On Fridays trains run until 2am; on Saturdays they roll through the night.

🚋 Tram

Bilbao's new tram system is a pleasure to use. It runs from the Atxuri train station to La Casilla at the other end of the city. Key stops include the Guggenheim, Teatro Arriaga and the Termibus station.

🚌 Bus

Bilbobus runs citywide bus services and has dozens of different lines, although in general most places of tourist interest are within walking distance of one another. In San Sebastián the most useful bus line for a tourist is bus 16, which travels from the city centre to Monte Igueldo.

Bilbao & San Sebastián
Neighbourhoods

Getxo & Portugalete (p54)
Joined by the Unesco-listed Puente Colgante, Getxo and Portugalete boast sandy beaches and excellent fish restaurants.

Worth a Trip
👁 **Top Sights**
Guernica
Central Basque Coast

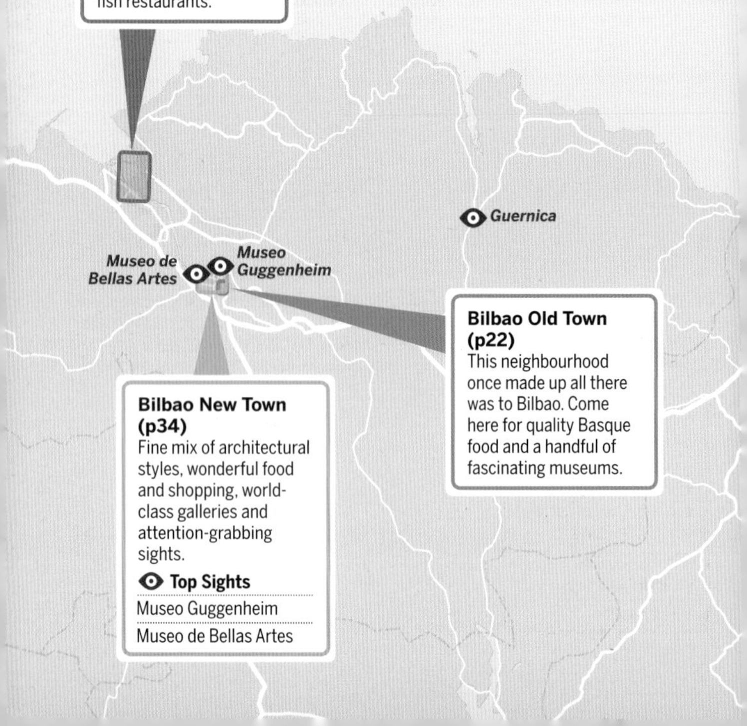

👁 Guernica

Museo de Bellas Artes 👁👁 *Museo Guggenheim*

Bilbao Old Town (p22)
This neighbourhood once made up all there was to Bilbao. Come here for quality Basque food and a handful of fascinating museums.

Bilbao New Town (p34)
Fine mix of architectural styles, wonderful food and shopping, world-class galleries and attention-grabbing sights.
👁 **Top Sights**
Museo Guggenheim
Museo de Bellas Artes

San Sebastián Parte Vieja (p70)
A compact nest of old streets containing the finest *pintxo* bars in all of Spain. Outside dining hours, the aquarium and museum will appeal.

👁 **Top Sights**

San Telmo Museoa

Aquarium

San Sebastián Gros (p102)
Hang on the beach with the surfers, admire the modern architecture of the Kursaal and devote yourself to discovering new culinary horizons.

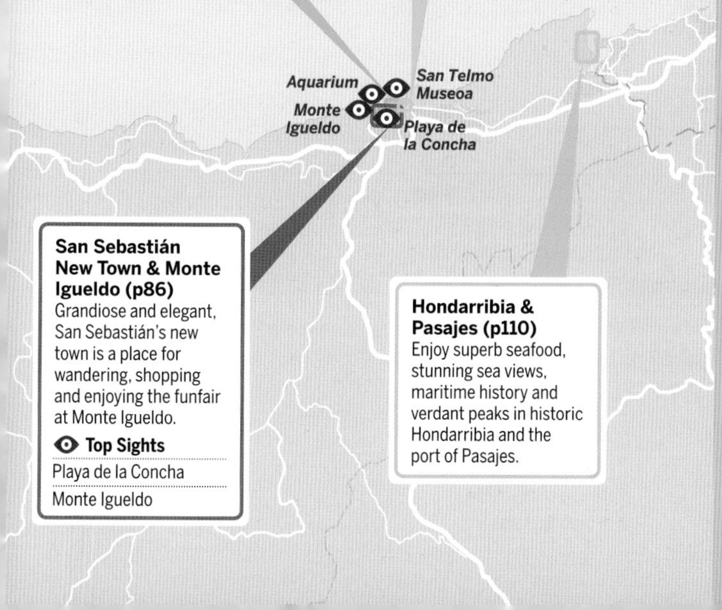

Aquarium

San Telmo Museoa

Monte Igueldo

Playa de la Concha

San Sebastián New Town & Monte Igueldo (p86)
Grandiose and elegant, San Sebastián's new town is a place for wandering, shopping and enjoying the funfair at Monte Igueldo.

👁 **Top Sights**

Playa de la Concha

Monte Igueldo

Hondarribia & Pasajes (p110)
Enjoy superb seafood, stunning sea views, maritime history and verdant peaks in historic Hondarribia and the port of Pasajes.

Explore
Bilbao & San Sebastián

Worth a Trip

Zubizuri (p46)
CHRISTOPHER RENNIE/GETTY IMAGES ©

Explore

Bilbao Old Town

The compact Casco Viejo, Bilbao's atmospheric old quarter, is full of charming streets, boisterous bars, quirky shops and fabulous cuisine. At the old town's heart are Bilbao's original seven streets, Las Siete Calles, which date from the 14th century and are the origin of the city as we know it today.

ALAN KRAFT/SHUTTERSTOCK ©

The Sights in a Day

The old town is full of history, so fortify yourself with caffeine, don your scholar's hat and start your exploration of Bilbao past and present outside the city's classiest theatre, the **Teatro Arriaga** (p30), which sits on the very edge of the old town. From here, wend your way through the fascinating web of narrow streets to the **Catedral de Santiago** (p25), subtle on the outside and impressive on the inside. Next, follow Calle de Iparragirre to the **Euskal Museoa** (p25), which is probably the world's most complete museum of Basque history and culture.

It's now time to join the locals for lunch at **Rio-Oja** (p26), one of Bilbao's typical working-class restaurants. Afterwards head back to the history books and the **Arkeologi Museo** (p25). Archaeology lesson complete, jump forward to the pleasures of today and a little shopping in the old town's varied boutiques.

As evening comes, everyone and anyone in Bilbao heads to the **Plaza Nueva** (p33) for *pintxos* (tapas) in one of half a dozen busy bars.

For a local's evening in the Old Town, see p32.

Local Life

Bar-Hopping in Bilbao (p32)

Best of Bilbao

Eating
Rio-Oja (p26)

Drinking & Nightlife
Teatro Arriaga (p30)

Shopping
Mercado de la Ribera (p31)

Almacen Coloniales y Bacalao Gregorio Martín (p31)

Vaho (p31)

Museums
Euskal Museoa (p25)

Arkeologi Museo (p25)

Getting There

Ⓜ **Metro** The Casco Viejo station will spit you out close to the Plaza Nueva and the museums.

🚊 **Tram** The Arriaga tram stop is by the Teatro Arriaga on the edge of the old town.

🚶 **Foot** Bilbao's a great walking city. From the Museo Guggenheim cross the river, turn right, and walk along the river for 15 minutes to the Plaza del Arenal and the old town.

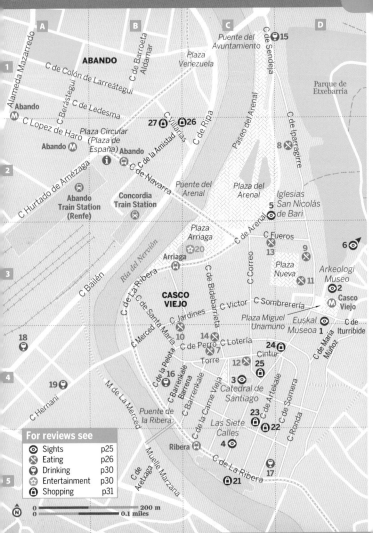

ABANDO

C de Colón de Larreátegui

Alameda Mazarredo

C de Berástegui

C de Barroeta Aldamar

Plaza Venezuela

Puente del Ayuntamiento

C de Sendeja

15

Parque de Etxebarria

Abando Ⓜ

C de Ledesma

C Lopez de Haro

Plaza Circular (Plaza de España)

27 🅐 26 🅐

C Villarías

C de Ripa

Paseo del Arenal

C de Iparragirre

8

Abando Ⓜ Abando

C de la Amistad

C de Navarra

C Hurtado de Amézaga

Abando Train Station (Renfe)

Concordia Train Station

Puente del Arenal

Plaza del Arenal

Iglesias San Nicolás de Bari

5

C de Arenal

C Fueros

6

Plaza Arriaga

Arriaga

20

Ría del Nervión

CASCO VIEJO

C de la Ribera

C de Bidebarrieta

C de Santa María

C Correo

13

9

Plaza Nueva

11

Arkeologi Museo

2

Casco Viejo Ⓜ

C de María Muñoz

C de Iturribide

C Bailén

C Jardines

10

C Merced Santa María

C de Perro

14

C Loteria

C Victor

C Sombrerería

Euskal Museoa 1

Plaza Miguel Unamuno

18

C de la Pelota

7

Torre

16

C Barrenkale Barrena

C Barrenkale

12

3

24

Cintur

25

23

22

C de Artekale

C de Somera

C Ronda

19

C Hernani

M de La Merced

C de la Carne Vieja

Catedral de Santiago

Las Siete Calles

Puente de la Ribera

Ribera

4

17

21

C de La Ribera

M de Arekaga

Muelle Marzana

C de Arekaga

0 ——————— 200 m
0 ——————— 0.1 miles

Ⓝ

Catedral de Santiago

Sights

Euskal Museoa   MUSEUM

1 Map p24, D3

This is probably the most complete
museum of Basque culture and history in all of Spain. The story begins
in prehistory; from this murky
period the displays bound rapidly
up to the modern age, in the process
explaining just how long the Basques
have called this corner of the world
home. (Museo Vasco; www.euskal-museoa.
org/es/hasiera; Plaza Miguel Unamuno 4;
adult/child €3/free, Thu free; ⊙10am-7pm
Mon & Wed-Fri, 10am-1.30pm & 4-7pm Sat,
10am-2pm Sun)

Arkeologi Museo   MUSEUM

2 Map p24, D3

Through the use of numerous flashing
lights, beeping things, and spearheads
and old pots, this museum reinforces
the point that the inhabitants of this
corner of Spain have lived here for a
very long time indeed. Labelling is in
Spanish and Basque only. (Calzadas de
Mallona 2; adult/student/child €3/1.50/free,
free Fri; ⊙10am-2pm & 4-7.30pm Tue-Sat,
10.30am-2pm Sun)

Catedral de Santiago   CATHEDRAL

3 Map p24, C4

Towering above all in the Casco Viejo
(although strangely invisible in the
narrow streets) is the Catedral de

Santiago, which has a pleasing cloister and Renaissance portico. The portico dates back to 1581; town councils were once held under it. (Plaza de Santiago; ⊘10am-1pm & 5-7.30pm Tue-Sat and 10am-1pm Sun & holidays)

Las Siete Calles
AREA

4 ◉ Map p24, C5

Forming the heart of Bilbao's Casco Viejo are seven streets known as the Siete Calles (Basque: Zazpi Kaleak). These dark, atmospheric lanes – Barrenkale Barrena, Barrenkale, Carnicería Vieja, Belostikale, Tendería, Artekale and Somera – date to the 1400s when the east bank of the Ría del Nervión was first developed. They originally constituted the city's commercial centre and river port; these days they teem with lively cafes, *pintxo* bars and boutiques.

Q Local Life

Parque Natural de Urkiola

Travelling between Bilbao and San Sebastián, it would be hard to miss the soaring mountain massif of the **Parque Natural de Urkiola** (www.urkiola.net; admission free; ⊘10am-2pm & 4-6pm Jun-Sep, shorter hours rest of year). The park, which consists of rolling meadows and pastures, sheer limestone mountain cliffs and pretty forests, is a favourite weekend bolt-hole for urbanites from both Bilbao and San Sebastián. The most popular activities are hiking, picnicking and rock climbing.

Iglesias San Nicolás de Bari
CHURCH

5 ◉ Map p24, C2

This landmark church by the northern entrance to the Casco Viejo was consecrated in 1756. Dedicated to St Nicholas of Bari, the patron saint of sailors, it features a baroque facade emblazoned with impressive heraldic stonework over the main portal and two bell towers. (Plaza de San Nicolás; ⊘10.30am-1pm & 5.30-7.30pm Mon-Sat)

Basilica de Begoña
BASILICA

6 ◉ Map p24, D3

This 16th-century basilica towers over the Casco Viejo from atop a nearby hill. It's mainly Gothic in look, although Renaissance touches, such as the arched main entrance, crept in during its century-long construction. The austere vaulted interior is brightened by a gold altarpiece which contains a statue of the Virgin Begoña, the patron saint of Biscay who's venerated locally as Amatxu (Mother). (Calle Virgen de Begoña; ⊘8.30am-1.30pm & 5-8.30pm Mon-Sat, 9am-2pm & 5-9pm Sun)

Eating

Rio-Oja
BASQUE €

7 ◉ Map p24, C4

An institution that shouldn't be missed. It specialises in light Basque seafood and heavy inland fare, but for most visitors the snails, sheep brains or squid floating in pools of ink are

Understand
Lauburu

The most visible symbol of Basque culture is the *lauburu*, or Basque cross. You'll see dozens of beautiful old examples of them inside the Euskal Museoa in Bilbao. *Lauburu* means 'four heads' in Basque and it's so named because of the four comma-like heads. The meaning of this symbol is lost in the misty past – some say it represents the four old regions of the Basque country, others that it represents spirit, life, consciousness and form – but today many regard it as a symbol of prosperity. It's also used to signify life and death and so is found on old headstones. Another theory as to its meaning is that it originally started appearing on 16th-century tombstones to indicate the grave of a healer of animals and souls (similar to a spiritual healer). When all is said and done, however, there's no real proof for any of these arguments.

the makings of a culinary adventure story they'll be recounting for years. Don't worry, though: it really does taste much better than it sounds. (944 15 08 71; www.rio-oja.com; Calle de Perro 4; mains €7-12; 9am-11pm Tue-Sun)

Claudio: La Feria del Jamón
PINTXOS €

8 Map p24, D2

A creaky old place full of ancient furnishings. As you'll guess from the name and the legs of cured ham hanging from the ceiling, it's all about pigs and cheap wine. Opposite the bar is a shop selling hams. (Calle lparragirre 9-18; pintxos from €2.50; 10am-2pm & 5-9pm Mon-Fri, 10am-2pm & 6-9.30pm Sat)

Bar Gure Toki
PINTXOS €

9 Map p24, D3

With a subtle but simple line in creative *pintxos* including some made with ostrich. (Plaza Nueva 12; pintxos from €2.50)

Berton Sasibil
PINTXOS €

10 Map p24, B4

Watch films about the creation of the *pintxos* that you're munching on. It also serves full meals, but these are nowhere near in the same league. (Calle Jardines 8; pintxos from €2.50; 8.30am-midnight Mon-Sat, 10am-4pm Sun)

Casa Victor Montes
BASQUE €€

11 Map p24, D3

Part bar, part shop, part restaurant and total work of art, the Victor Montes is quite touristy, but locals also appreciate its over-the-top decoration, good food and the 1000 or so bottles of wine. If you're stopping by for a full meal, book in advance and savour the house special, *bacalao* (salted cod). (944 15 70 67; www.victor montesbilbao.com; Plaza Nueva 8; mains €15, pintxos from €2.50; 10.30am-11pm Mon-Thu, 10.30am-midnight Fri & Sun)

Understand

The Art of Eating Pintxos

Just rolling the word *pintxo* (peen-cho) around your tongue defines the essence of this cheerful, cheeky little slice of Basque cuisine. The perfect *pintxo* should have exquisite taste, texture and appearance and should be savoured in two elegant bites. The Basque version of a tapa, the *pintxo* transcends the commonplace by the sheer panache of its culinary campiness.

Many *pintxos* are bedded on small pieces of bread or on tiny half-baguettes, upon which towering creations are constructed. Some bars specialise in seafood, with much use of marinated anchovies, prawns and strips of squid, all topped with anything from chopped crab to pâté. Others deal in pepper or mushroom delicacies, or simply offer a mix of everything. And the choice isn't normally limited to what's on the bar top in front of you: many of the best *pintxos* are the hot ones you need to order.

For many visitors, ordering *pintxos* can seem like one of the dark arts of Spanish etiquette. Fear not: in many bars in Bilbao and San Sebastián, it couldn't be easier. With so many *pintxos* varieties lined up along the bar, you either take a small plate and help yourself or point to the morsel you want. Otherwise, many places have a list of *pintxos*, either on a menu or posted up behind the bar. If you can't choose, ask for '*la especialidad de la casa*' (the house specialty) and it's hard to go wrong. Another way of eating *pintxos* is to order *raciones* (literally 'rations'; large *pintxos* servings) or *media raciones* (half-rations; bigger plates than tapas servings but smaller than standard *raciones*). These plates and half-plates of a particular dish are a good way to go if you particularly like something and want more than a mere *pintxo*. Remember, however, that after a couple of *raciones* most people are full.

A couple of other points to remember. Most locals prefer to just have one or two *pintxos* in each bar before moving on to the next place. Ordering half a dozen different *pintxos* just for yourself is the mark of a tourist. And remember, despite popular belief, *pintxos* are never free. In fact the cost of a few mouthfuls can quickly add up.

ANNE RIPPY/GETTY IMAGES ©

Teatro Arriaga (p30)

Baster

PINTXOS €

 12 Map p24, C4

A relaxed and popular bar, Baster serves a range of classic *pintxos*, many featuring locally caught anchovies and sardines, and fine *txakoli* (the local white wine). It gets very busy at weekend lunchtimes when bar-hoppers crowd its pavement tables and bright, modern interior. (Calle Correo 22; pintxos €1.50-6.50; ⏰9.30am-10pm Tue-Thu, to 11.30pm Fri & Sat, to 3.30pm Sun)

Los Fueros

BASQUE €€

13 Map p24, C3

Seafood stars at this backstreet bar-restaurant near Plaza Nueva, appearing in time-honoured crowd-pleasers like grilled prawns and fried hake with pepper mayonnaise. The bar is smarter than many old town places, decked out in contemporary mosaic-tiling and cool Mediterranean blues. (☎944 15 30 47; www.losfueros.com; Calle Fueros 6; pintxos €5-6, mains €12-16; ⏰noon-midnight Mon & Wed-Sat, to 4pm Tue & Sun)

El Txoko Berria

BASQUE €€

 14 Map p24, C4

This welcoming restaurant is a good bet for honest, earthy local cuisine. Take a seat in the handsome dining room and dig into staples such as cod Bizkaina style (with a sweet, slightly spicy pepper sauce)

and grilled meats. (📞944 79 42 98; www.eltxokoberria.com; Calle de Bidebarrieta 14; mains €8-16; 🕐1-4pm & 7.30-11pm)

Drinking

Opila
CAFE

15 🚇 Map p24, D1

Fantastic patisserie and cafe. Downstairs is all art deco furnishings and glass display cabinets; upstairs is way more up to the moment. It's the perfect breakfast spot close to the old town and its hot chocolate pleases at any time of day. (Calle de Sendeja 4)

Lamiak
CAFE

16 🚇 Map p24, B4

Lamiak, a long-standing Casco Viejo favourite, is a buzzing cafe with a cavernous red and black hall, cast-iron columns and upstairs seating on a mezzanine floor. Good for coffees and cocktails, it exudes an arty, laid-back vibe and pulls in a cool weekend crowd. (Calle Pelota 8; 🕐4pm-midnight Sun-Thu, 3.30pm-2.30am Fri & Sat)

K2
BAR

17 🚇 Map p24, C5

One of a number of lively drinking haunts on Calle Somera, K2 is a modest tunnel-shaped bar frequented by a young, studenty crowd, particularly at weekends when it stays open into the small hours. There are *pintxos*, but most people prefer to hang out outside sipping on pints and glasses of local

wine. (Calle Somera 10; 🕐9am-midnight Mon-Fri, noon-3am Sat, to 2am Sun)

El Balcón de la Lola
CLUB

18 🚇 Map p24, A4

One of Bilbao's most popular mixed gay/straight clubs, this is the place to come if you're looking for hip industrial decor and a packed Saturday-night disco. It's located under the railway lines. (Calle Bailén 10; admission Fri & Sat €8-10; 🕐11.45pm-6.15am Thu & Fri, noon-3.30pm & 11.45pm-6.15am Sat, noon-4.30pm Sun)

Badulake
CLUB

19 🚇 Map p24, A4

A well-known address on Bilbao's nightlife scene, Badulake bursts to life on Thursdays when Las Fellini, a local cabaret act, ham it up in front of a largely gay audience. On Friday and Saturday nights the fun is fuelled by '80s disco, mainstream pop and DJ-spun electronica. (www.badulakebilbao.com; Calle Hernani 10; 🕐9.30pm-5am Thu, to 6am Fri, midnight-6am Sat)

Entertainment

Teatro Arriaga
THEATRE

20 Map p24, C3

The baroque facade of this venue commands the open spaces of El Arenal between the Casco Viejo and the river. It stages theatrical performances and classical-music concerts. (📞944 79 20 36; www.teatroarriaga.com; Plaza Arriaga)

Shopping

Mercado de la Ribera   MARKET

21 🔒 Map p24, C5

Overlooking the river, this is supposedly one of the largest covered food markets in Spain. It's had a recent makeover which has sanitised it somewhat, but many of the city's top chefs still come here to select fresh produce each morning. (Calle de la Rilbera)

Almacen Coloniales y Bacalao Gregorio Martín   FOOD

22 🔒 Map p24, C4

Specialising in *bacalao* (salted cod) since it first opened some 80 years ago. Today it also sells oils, pulses and hams. (Calle Artekale 32; ⏲10am-2pm & 4-8pm Mon-Sat)

Txorierri   FOOD

23 🔒 Map p24, C4

High-quality deli selling the full tummy-pleasing array of local culinary delicacies. (Calle Artekale 19; ⏲10am-2pm & 4-8pm Mon-Sat)

Elkar Megadenda   BOOKS

24 🔒 Map p24, D4

Basque publications are strongly represented here. It also stocks books in Spanish and a few in English, and there's an excellent map and travel section. There are a couple of other branches in the city. (www.elkar.eus; Calle de Iparragirre 26; ⏲10am-2pm & 4.30-8pm

Mon-Sat Jul & Aug, 9.30am-8pm Mon-Fri, 10am-2pm & 5-8pm Sat Sep-Jun)

Vaho   ACCESSORIES

25 🔒 Map p24, C4

Street fashion goes green at this hip bag store where everything is made from material recycled from old advertising banners. The resulting satchels, messenger bags, wallets and the like are bright and bold with loud, in-your-face designs. (www.vaho.ws; Calle Correo 25; ⏲11am-2.30pm & 5-8.30pm Mon-Sat)

Persuade   FASHION

26 🔒 Map p24, C2

Housed in a former warehouse, complete with exposed brick walls, timber beams and cast-iron columns, this historic shop stocks the latest fashions by top international designers such as Comme des Garçons and Issey Miyake. It also has a range of vintage hats and modish bags. (📞944 23 88 64; www.persuade.es; Calle Villarías 8; ⏲11am-9pm Mon-Sat)

Power Records   MUSIC

27 🔒 Map p24, B2

This record shop has long been point of reference for Bilbao's vinyl lovers. Its encyclopaedic collection runs the gamut from death metal to Shirley Bassey by way of salsa, jazz, rock, pop and blues. There are collectors' box sets, LPs, posters and CDs. (📞944 24 55 90; www.powerrecordsbilbao.com; Calle Villarías 4; ⏲10.30am-2pm & 4.30-8pm Mon-Sat)

Local Life
Bar-Hopping in Bilbao

Getting There

Ⓜ **Metro** The Casco
Viejo station is the
starting point of this
bar-hopping extrava-
ganza on Plaza Nueva.

Perhaps the real highlight of a visit to Bilbao is the
simple pleasure of savouring an oaky Rioja and
nibbling on an artful *pintxo* (the Basque word for
tapas) in one of the city's many bars. This is an
experience best conducted with friends, hopping
from bar to bar, sipping wine and arguing over
which one serves the finest food.

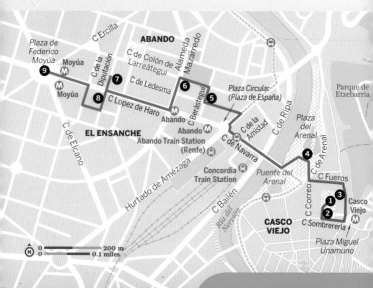

❶ Plaza Nueva

The **Plaza Nueva** is lined with *pintxo* bars, children racing around and adults catching up on the gossip over a drink and a tasty titbit. On Sunday mornings a flea market takes place – come here in search of old records, books, postcards, crockery and all manner of assorted odds and ends.

❷ Cafe-Bar Bilbao

Asking a group of locals to pick a favourite bar on the Plaza Nueva is a sure-fire way of starting an argument. Start your exploration of the square's culinary skills at the **Cafe-Bar Bilbao** (Plaza Nueva 6; pintxos from €2.50; ⏰7am-11pm Mon-Fri, 9am-11.30pm Sat, 10am-3pm Sun) with its cool blue southern tiles, warm northern atmosphere and superb array of *pintxos*.

❸ Sorginzulo

Each bar in the Plaza Nueva has a devoted following and house special. The **Sorginzulo** (Plaza Nueva 12; pintxos from €2.50; ⏰9.30am-12.30am) is a matchbox-sized place with an exemplary spread. The house special is calamari (squid), but it's only served at the weekend.

❹ Plaza del Arenal

The morphing ground between the Casco Viejo and the newer parts of Bilbao, the **Plaza del Arenal** is a large open space that frequently plays host to outdoor exhibitions and on Sunday mornings is home to a sweet-smelling flower market.

❺ Museo del Vino

The white-tiled interior and Gaudí-esque windows of the **Museo del Vino** (Calle de Ledesma 10; pintxos from €2.50; ⏰1-5pm & 8-11pm Mon-Fri) combine with delicious octopus *pintxos* and, no surprise here, an excellent wine list.

❻ Bitoque de Albia

The award-winning **Bitoque de Albia** (www.bitoque.net; Alameda Mazarredo 6; pintxos from €2.50; ⏰1.30-4pm Mon-Wed, 1.30-4pm & 8.30-11.15pm Thu-Sat) serves up clever creations such as miniature red tuna burgers, salmon sushi and clams with wild mushrooms. It also offers a *pintxos* tasting menu (€12).

❼ Los Candiles

A narrow, low-key bar, **Los Candiles** (Calle de Diputación 1; pintxos from €2.50; ⏰7am-10pm Mon-Sat) serves up subtle snacks filled with the taste of the sea.

❽ El Globo

The unassuming **El Globo** (www.barel globo.com; Calle de Diputación 8; pintxos from €2.50; ⏰8am-11pm Mon-Thu, 8am-midnight Fri & Sat) has favourites such as *txangurro gratinadao* (spider crab).

❾ Plaza de Federico Moyúa

With its fountains and spinning traffic, **Plaza de Federico Moyúa** (Plaza Mayor) is the heart of the Ensanche and as good a place as any to finish this food-and-drink-drenched amble. The plaza is home to the regal Hotel Carlton; once the hotel of choice for luminaries such as Einstein and Hemingway.

Explore

Bilbao New Town

Bilbao's elegant new town has an impressive roster of attractions, and it's likely you'll spend a lot of time here. The neighbourhood is home to several world-class museums, beautiful river views and walks, some of the best restaurants and bars in Spain, and plenty of interesting, quirky diversions.

The Sights in a Day

☀ Start at the building that made the city famous: the **Museo Guggenheim** (p36). Don't forget to devote plenty of time to exploring the exterior and surrounding riverbanks. The Guggenheim will likely take up much of your morning, so afterwards head straight to lunch either at the in-house **Nerua** (p48) or **La Mary Restaurante** (p49).

☼ After lunch, unwind with a walk through the peaceful **Parque de Doña Casilda de Iturrizar** (p44) before re-engaging with more art – this time the works of Spanish masters in the **Museo de Bellas Artes** (p40). If you're not suffering museum overload, double back and sail on over to the **Museo Marítimo Ría de Bilbao** (p44). Otherwise, browse the shops along Calle Lopez de Haro and surrounding streets, stopping for a snack at the divine pastry shop **Arrese** (p52).

☽ In the evening, grab some choice *pintxos* at **La Viña del Ensanche** (p47) and then see what's on at the alternative Basque cultural centre **Kafe Antzokia** (p52).

👁 Top Sights

Museo Guggenheim Bilbao (p36)

Museo de Bellas Artes (p40)

💜 Best of Bilbao

Eating
La Viña del Ensanche (p47)

Agape Restaurante (p47)

Casa Rufo (p46)

Drinking & Nightlife
Kafe Antzokia (p52)

Euskalduna Palace (p52)

Café Iruña (p50)

Architecture
Museo Guggenheim Bilbao (p36)

Azkuna Zentroa (p44)

Concordia Train Station (p45)

Getting There

Ⓜ **Metro** Useful metro stations include Moyúa, which gets you bang into the heart of town, Abando for shopping, and San Mamés for the bus station.

🚊 **Tram** The tram runs along the length of the river with a stop close to the Museo Guggenheim Bilbao.

🚶 **Foot** It's a five-minute walk from the Guggenheim to the city centre.

Top Sights
Museo Guggenheim Bilbao

Opened in September 1997, Bilbao's shimmering titanium Museo Guggenheim is one of modern architecture's most iconic buildings. It almost single-handedly lifted Bilbao out of its post-industrial depression and into the 21st century – and with sensation. It boosted the city's inspired regeneration, stimulated further development and placed Bilbao firmly in the international art and tourism spotlight.

For many travellers, this extraordinary building is the primary reason for visiting Bilbao.

Map p42, E1

www.guggenheim
-bilbao.es

Avenida Abandoibarra 2

adult/student/child
€13/7.50/free

10am-8pm, closed
Mon Sep-Jun

Don't Miss

The Design

For most, it's the architecture itself that is the real star of the Guggenheim show. Designed by Frank Gehry, the Guggenheim's flowing canopies, promontories, ship-like shapes, towers and flying fins all covered in shimmering titanium tiles is irresistible. Allow plenty of time to walk around the exterior, observing how the patterns and colours change with the light.

Puppy

Outside, on the city side of the museum, is Jeff Koons' kitsch whimsy *Puppy*, a 12m tall highland terrier made up of thousands of flowers. Originally a temporary exhibition, Bilbao has hung on to 'El Poop'. *Bilbaínos* will tell you that El Poop came first – and then they built a kennel behind it.

Maman

On the riverbank just outside the Guggenheim is Louise Bourgeois' *Maman*: a skeletal spider-like canopy said to symbolise a protective embrace.

Atrium

The atrium, a huge cathedral-like space, serves as your first taste of the museum's interior. Light pours into this entrance gallery through what appear to be glass cliffs; at one end phrases of light reach for the skies. The atrium was designed to provide views of the river and surrounding hills.

Temporary Exhibitions

Temporary exhibitions can be extremely varied and over the years the museum has hosted exhibitions of Gucci clothing designs, works by Jeff Koons, recycled waste collections and reality distorting mirrors.

☑ Top Tips

▶ The Artean Pass (€14) is a joint ticket for the Museo de Bellas Artes and the Guggenheim, offering significant savings. It's available at both museums.

▶ Entry queues can be very long on wet summer days and around Easter. Try and visit at a different time or come early.

▶ Purchasing advance tickets online allows you to skip entry queues.

▶ For a bird's-eye perspective of the Guggenheim, ride the Funicular de Artxanda (p44) to the park high above the city.

✗ Take a Break

Head to the Guggenheim's Nerua (p48) restaurant for top-quality Basque cuisine. For something cheaper and less formal, try the in-house **Bistró** (menús from €19.50; ⊘1.30-3.30pm & 8-10.30pm).

Understand
The Vision Behind the Masterpiece

Designed by celebrated architect Frank Gehry, the Guggenheim dominates the Bilbao waterfront, its look and mood changing with the rising and falling light. The building sits on the grounds of a former industrial wasteland and the city's shipping, industrial and fishing heritage is evoked in its form, which some describe as resembling a ship or shimmering fish.

After the collapse of shipping and heavy industry in Bilbao, the authorities embarked on a regeneration of the city. One of the key requirements was a world-class cultural exhibition space, and from that idea came the Guggenheim. Since its opening in 1997, the museum has done much to transform Bilbao from run-down industrial city to a bona fide cultural hub. As well as playing off the city's historical and geographical context, the building also reflects Gehry's own interests, not least his engagement with industrial materials. The gleaming titanium tiles that sheathe most of the building like giant herring scales are said to have been inspired by the architect's childhood fascination with fish.

The Matter of Time

The ground floor of the Guggenheim is devoted to permanent exhibitions. One of the most popular with visitors is Richard Serra's rust-red steel *The Matter of Time*. Despite the grand name, this is best described as a giant steel maze, which often seems to serve as much as a children's playground as a work of art.

Tulips

From the atrium head out onto the little terrace surrounded by shallow pools of water to see Jeff Koons' *Tulips*, whose bubbly, colourful form represents a bouquet of giant balloon flowers (more than 2m tall and 5m across). The work belongs to his ambitious Celebration series.

Fog Sculpture #08025 (F.O.G.)

Outside the museum, lying between the glass buttresses of the central atrium and Ría del Nervión, is a simple pool of water that regularly emits a mist installation by Fuyiko Nakaya.

In case you missed the play on words here, FOG are also the initials of the building's architect.

Fountain

In the open area to the west of the museum, a fountain sculpture randomly fires off jets of water into the air while the young at heart leap to and fro across it. Nearby is an impressive children's play park.

Jeff Koons' *Puppy* (p37)

Waking

While some of the conceptual art in the Guggenheim is sometimes hard to fathom, Gilbert and George's *Waking* is a bright and bold piece that, on the surface at least, is easily accessible. It represents the passage from boyhood to maturity.

Lightning with Stag in its Glare

Created by German artist Joseph Beuys, the suspended bronze triangle represents a bolt of lightning illumin-ating various startled animals. The three-wheeled cart represents a goat and the upended ironing board a stag.

Tall Tree & the Eye

Outside the museum is Anish Kapoor's work, *Tall Tree & the Eye*. It consists of 73 reflective spheres anchored around three axes, each of which distorts real-ity as you look into it.

Top Sights
Museo de Bellas Artes

The city's fine arts museum might not have the glitz and glamour of its more famous cousin, but the truth is that many people rate the exhibits here higher than those in the Guggenheim. Collections range from works by well-known masters such as Goya and El Greco to pieces by more modern artists.

👁 Map p42, D2

www.museobilbao.com

Plaza del Museo 2

adult/student/child €7/5/free, Wed free

🕙10am-8pm Wed-Mon

Don't Miss

Classical Collection

The heart of the museum's huge collection of art (some 10,000 pieces) consists of the classical collection, with works dating from the 12th to 19th centuries. Show-stoppers include Murillo's *Saint Peter in Tears*, which depicts St Peter at the moment of his repentance. El Greco's *The Annunciation* also draws crowds, as does Goya's *Portrait of Martín Zapater*.

Contemporary Collection

Stars of the contemporary collection, which covers the period from the 20th century on-wards, include Paul Gauguin's *Laveuses à Arles*, which depicts washerwomen in Arles, France, where Gauguin lived for a time, and Francis Bacon's *Lying Figure in a Mirror*, which shows, in a rather abstract way, a male figure reflected in a mirror.

Basque Collection

The Basque Country's finest art gallery wouldn't be complete without a comprehensive body of work from the region's best-known artists. This includes sculptor Eduardo Chillida's *Trembling Irons*, which was one of the pieces that brought him to worldwide attention. Ignacio Zuloaga and Juan de Echevarría are also represented.

Temporary Exhibitions

The permanent collection of the Museo de Bellas Artes is one of the finest in Spain outside of Madrid, but the temporary exhibitions are what draw the crowds. See the website for details of upcoming exhibitions.

ALLAN BAXTER/GETTY IMAGES ©

☑ Top Tips

▶ The Artean Pass (€14) is a joint ticket for the Museo de Bellas Artes and the Guggenheim, offering significant savings. It's available at both museums.

▶ Queues for temporary exhibitions can be very long. Buy an advance ticket online.

▶ Learn more by picking up an audio guide (€2) at the museum entrance.

▶ After you've enjoyed the art, reflect on all you've seen in the neighbouring Parque de Doña Casilda de Iturrizar (p44).

✕ Take a Break

The in-house **Arbola-gaña Restaurant** (meals €60; ⏱1.30-3.30pm & 9-10.30pm Thu-Sat, 1.30-3.30pm Sun, Tue & Wed) offers high-class cuisine that's every bit as creative as the art on display. For cheaper fare, head to the museum's **cafe** (snacks €8-10) for salads, sand-wiches and *pintxos*.

A   B   C   D

N   0 ⊢——————————⊣ 500 m
    0 ⊢——————————⊣ 0.25 miles

1

Ría del Nervión

30 🔒 Av Abandoibarra

Abandoibarra

Guggenl

2

Museo Marítimo
Ría de Bilbao ◉**1**

⭐ **26**

Euskalduna

Plaza del
Museo

Alameda

3◉ Parque de
Doña Casilda
de Iturrizar
◉

*Museo de
Bellas Artes*
◉

C de Elcand

23 📍

C de Máximo Aguirre

Gran Vía de Don Diego

3

Sabino
Arana Ⓜ

C de Rodríguez Arias

Plaza de
Campuzano

San Mamés Ⓜ

Av de Sabino Arana

Alameda de Urquijo

18 ❌

C de Licenciado Poza

⊗**20**

⊗**21**

C Ercilla

28
🔒

Termibus

C de Luis Briñas

C de María Díaz de Haro

Alameda del Doctor Areilza

Indautxu
Ⓜ

Plaza de
Indautxu

Alameda de Urquijo

Azkuna Zentroa
(Alhóndiga)
◉**4**

C de Recalde

4 🅿

C Manuel Allende

C de Gregorio
de la Revilla

🔒**24**

Plaza de
Echaniz

Alameda de San Mamés

17

5

La Casilla

Plaza
de la
Casilla

Av de la Autonomía

Museo Taurino
de Bilbao
◉**6**

For reviews see	
◉ Top Sights	p36
◉ Sights	p44
❌ Eating	p46
🍷 Drinking	p51
⭐ Entertainment	p52
🔒 Shopping	p52

E

Museo Guggenheim 👁

im 🍽15

ⓘ Mazarredo

C Lersundi

C Barraincua

🏨22

C de los Heros

C de Cosme Echevarrieta

Alameda de Recalde

C de Henao

C Ercilla

ABANDO

🍽16

Plaza de Jado

C de Colón de Larreátegui

Plaza del Ensanche

Plaza de Federico Moyúa

Ⓜ Moyúa

Ⓜ Moyúa

🔒29

🔒27

C de Ledesma

🛍13

C de la Diputación

C Lopez de Haro Ⓜ

🛍11

C de Elcano

EL ENSANCHE

C de General Concha

C de Eibalduna

Hurtado de Amézaga

🛍9

C de Garcia Salazar

Plaza de Zabalburu

F

/ Bilbao Airport (11km)

C Huertas de la Villa

Paseo Campo Volantin

Uribitarte 🚇

🚊19

🏛8 Zubizuri

C de Uribitarte

C San Vicente

⭐25

C de Berástegui

Plaza Circular (Plaza de España)

C de Buenos Aires

Abando Ⓜ

Abando Train Station (Renfe) 🚉

Concordia 👁5 Train Station

C Bailén

C Hernani

🍽10 🍽12

G

Funicular de Artxanda

C Castaños

2 👁

Río del Nervión

7 Bilboats

🚇 Pio Baroja

14 🏛

C de Barroeta Aldamar

Plaza Venezuela

C Villarias

C de Ripa

🚉 Abando

C de Navarra

Plaza del Arenal

Puente del Arenal

Plaza Arriaga

🚉 Arriaga

C de Arenal

Plaza Nueva

CASCO VIEJO

C de La Ribera

🚉 Ribera

H

Av Maurice Ravel

1

Av Zumalacárregui

2

Puente del Ayuntamiento

Parque de Etxebarria

3

C de Iparragirre

Casco Ⓜ Viejo

4

5

Sights

Museo Marítimo Ría de Bilbao

MUSEUM

1 ◎ Map p42, B2

This space-age maritime museum, appropriately sited down on the waterfront, uses bright and well-thought-out displays to bring the watery depths of Bilbao and Basque maritime history to life. There's an outdoor section where children (and nautically inclined grown-ups) can clamber about a range of boats pretending to be pirates and sailors, in addition to frequent temporary exhibitions. (www.museomaritimobilbao.org; Muelle Ramón de la Sota 1; adult/student & child/under 6yr €6/3.50/free; ⊙10am-8pm Tue-Sun, closes earlier Tues Oct-Mar)

Local Life

Parque Natural de Gorbeia

Home to Mt Gorbeia (1481m), south of Bilbao, this natural park contains diverse and stimulating landscapes. As well as the rounded dome of Gorbeia itself, there's a vast maze-like landscape of karst rock formations and mysterious caves filled with legends. There are numerous hiking trails here and some beautiful picnic spots. Access is via Pagomakurre, where you'll find an **information centre** (⊙10am-2pm & 4-6pm Jun-Sep, shorter hours rest of year). You'll need a car to get here.

Funicular de Artxanda

FUNICULAR

2 ◎ Map p42, G1

Bilbao is a city hemmed in by hills and mountains, resting in a tight valley. For a breathtaking view over the city and the wild Basque mountains beyond, take a trip on the funicular railway that has creaked and moaned its way up the steep slope to the summit of Artxanda for nearly a century. (Plaza Funicular; adult/child €0.95/0.31; ⊙7.15am-11pm Mon-Sat, 8.15am-10pm Sun Jun-Sep, closes earlier Oct-May)

Parque de Doña Casilda de Iturrizar

PARK

3 ◎ Map p42, C2

Floating on waves of peace and quiet just beyond the Museo de Bellas Artes is another work of fine art – the Parque de Doña Casilda de Iturrizar. The centrepiece of this whimsical park is the large pond filled with ornamental ducks and other waterfowl.

Azkuna Zentroa (Alhóndiga)

ARCHITECTURE

4 ◎ Map p42, D4

Take a neglected wine storage warehouse, convert it into a leisure and cultural centre, add a bit of Bilbao style and the result is the Azkuna Zentroa (Alhóndiga). Designed by renowned architect Philippe Starck, it now houses cinemas, a rooftop swimming pool with a glass bottom,

Concordia train station

cafes and restaurants. The ground floor is notable for its tubby pillars that look like they've been squashed under the weight of the rest of the building. (www.azkunazentroa.com; Plaza Alhóndiga 4)

Concordia Train Station

LANDMARK

5 Map p42, G4

The Concordia train station, with its handsome art nouveau facade of wrought iron and tiles, was built in 1902 and for many years provided colour and interest in a city once known only for industrial decay. (Estación de Santander; Calle Lopez de Haro)

Museo Taurino de Bilbao

MUSEUM

6 Map p42, D5

Although Bilbao isn't a bullfighting city in the manner of the towns of Andalucía, the audiences here are considered by matadors to be among the most discerning and hardest to please. The city's bullring, an ugly 1960s looking lump of concrete that brings to mind the industrial Bilbao of old, houses a small museum dedicated to the bulls and the local history of the fight.

The collection includes elaborate matador outfits and hundreds of bullfight posters. (Plaza de Toros Vista Alegre;

adult/child €3/free; ⏱10am-1.30pm & 4-6pm Mon-Thu, 10am-1.30pm Fri)

Bilboats
BOAT TOUR

7 ◉ Map p42, G3

Runs boat cruises along Bilbao's Ría del Nervión several times a day. (☎946 42 41 57; www.bilboats.com; Plaza Pío Baroja; adult/child from €12/7)

Zubizuri
BRIDGE

8 ◉ Map p42, G2

The most striking of the modern bridges that span the Ría del Nervión, the Zubizuri (Basque for 'White Bridge') has become an iconic feature of Bilbao's cityscape since its completion in 1997. Designed by Spanish architect Santiago Calatrava, it has a curved walkway suspended under a flowing white arch to which it's attached by a series of steel spokes.

Eating

Casa Rufo
BASQUE €€

9 ✖ Map p42, F4

Despite the emergence of numerous glitzy restaurants that are temples to haute cuisine, this resolutely old-fashioned place, with its shelves full of dusty bottles of top-quality olive oil and wine, still stands out as one of the best places to eat traditional Basque food in Bilbao. The house special is steak – lovingly cooked over hot coals.

NITO/SHUTTERSTOCK ©

Zubizuri

Understand

Athletic Bilbao

Watching a football match at the **Estadio San Mamés** (www.athletic-club.eus) is one of Bilbao's great experiences. The home side, Athletic Bilbao, is one of Spain's most successful clubs, and one of only three to have never been relegated from La Liga along with Real Madrid and Barcelona.

The club, founded in 1898 after British sailors introduced football to the city, inspires passionate local support and its traditional red and white colours are displayed in cafes and bars across town. But what sets it apart – and makes its achievements even more impressive – is its unique policy of only signing Basque players.

Tickets for games are available through the team's website, directly at the stadium or, on match days, from BKK cashpoint machines.

The restaurant also doubles as a deli and many of the products lining the shelves are for sale. Advance reservations are a good idea. (📞944 43 21 72; www.casarufo.com; Hurtado de Amézaga 5; mains €10-15; ⏰1.30-4pm & 8.30-11pm Mon-Sat)

Agape Restaurante
BASQUE €€

 10 Map p42, F5

With a solid reputation among locals for good-value meals that don't sacrifice quality, this is a great place for a slice of real Bilbao culinary life. It's well away from the standard tourist circuit, but is worth the short walk. (📞944 16 05 06; www.restauranteagape.com; Calle de Hernani 13; menú del día €12.20, menús €14.80-36; ⏰1-4pm Sun-Wed, 1-4pm & 8.30-11.30pm Thu-Sat)

La Viña del Ensanche
PINTXOS €

 11 Map p42, E3

Hundreds of bottles of wine line the walls of this outstanding octogenarian *pintxos* bar. This could very well be the best place to eat *pintxos* in the entire city. If you can't decide what to sample, opt for the €30 tasting menu. (📞944 15 56 15; www.lavinadelensanche.com; Calle de la Diputación 10; pintxos from €2.50, menú €30; ⏰8.30am-11pm Mon-Fri, noon-1am Sat)

Mina Restaurante
CONTEMPORARY BASQUE €€€

 12 Map p42, G5

Offering unexpected sophistication and fine dining in an otherwise fairly grimy neighbourhood, this riverside restaurant has some critics citing it as the current numero uno in Bilbao.

Expect serious culinary creativity: think along the lines of spider crab with passion fruit or frozen 'seawater' with seaweed and lemon sorbet Reservations are essential. (☎944 79 59 38; www.restaurantemina.es; Muelle Marzana; tasting menus €60-110; ⏰2-3.30pm & 9-10.30pm Wed-Sat, 2-3.30pm Sun & Tue)

El Globo   PINTXOS €

14 ✗ Map p42, E3

This is a popular bar with a terrific range of *pintxos modernos,* including favourites such as *txangurro gratinado* (spider crab) and *hongos con su crema y crujiente de jamón* (mushrooms with crusted ham). Its variety, congenial atmosphere and central location mean that many locals regard it as one of the best around. (www.barelglobo.com; Calle de Diputación 8; pintxos from €2.50; ⏰8am-11pm Mon-Thu, 8am-midnight Fri & Sat)

Bascook   CONTEMPORARY BASQUE €€€

14 ✗ Map p42, G3

The style of this unique place won't appeal to all. The lighting is more nightclub than restaurant and the menu is printed in the form of a newspaper, but even if the decor doesn't do it for you the food probably will: an utterly modern take on Basque classics mixed with hints of far-off lands. It's very popular with locals. (☎944 00 99 77; www.bascook.com; Calle de Barroeta Aldamar 8; menú del día €24, menús €50-60, mains €12-18; ⏰lunch Mon-Sat, dinner Thu-Sat)

Nerua Guggenheim
Bilbao   CONTEMPORARY BASQUE €€€

15 ✗ Map p42, E1

The Guggenheim's modernist, chic and very white restaurant is under the direction of Michelin-starred chef Josean Alija (a disciple of Ferran Adrià). Needless to say, the *nueva*

Understand
Bilbao's Metro

Bilbao's architectural riches run deep. Walk across town and you'll come across a number of futuristic glass-and-steel constructions emerging from the ground. Nicknamed *fosteritos* after Sir Norman Foster, the British architect who designed and built them between 1988 and 1995, these are the entrances to the city's metro stations.

Bilbao's metro system is a masterpiece of modern functional design. Stations are cavernous and clean, and with only two lines, it's a doddle to use. Get your ticket from the touchscreen machines near the barriers, go through and head right or left down to your platform. Simple as that.

Yandiola (p50)

cocina vasca (Basque nouvelle cuisine) is breathtaking – even the olives are vintage classics: all come from 1000-year-old trees!

Reservations are essential. If the gourmet restaurant is too extravagant for you, try the **Bistró** (p37), which has *menús* from €20. (📞944 00 04 30; www.neruaguggenheimbilbao.com; tasting menu from €65, mains €30-35; ⏱1-3pm & 8.30-9.30pm Thu-Sat, 1-3pm Tue, Wed & Sun)

Zortziko Restaurante

CONTEMPORARY BASQUE €€€

16 🍴 Map p42, F2

Michelin-starred chef Daniel García presents immaculate modern Basque cuisine in a formal 1920s-style French dining room. The highly inventive menu changes frequently, but might include such delicacies as grilled scallops with liquid potatoes and truffles or, and here's one you don't see cropping up all that much, pigeon ice cream.

If the food inspires your taste buds, then sign up for one of his occasional cooking courses (€40). (📞944 23 97 43; www.zortziko.es; Alameda Mazarredo 17; *menús* from €85, mains €22-39; ⏱1-3.30pm & 9.30-11pm Tue-Sat; 🖊)

La Mary Restaurante

BASQUE €

17 🍴 Map p42, D4

From the outside this looks like quite a swanky place, but in fact it's very casual. To enjoy the bargain lunch *menú* you'll need to arrive early; otherwise, count on joining the queue of locals waiting for a table. It might not be the best quality in town, but it's probably the best value. (www.lamaryrestaurant.com; Plaza de Arriquíbar 3; menú del día €10, mains €8-10; ⏱1-4pm & 8-11.30pm)

Mugi
PINTXOS €

18 Map p42, C3

For more than 50 years this highly regarded *pintxos* bar has been serving up over 40 different kinds of *pintxos*. Its popularity means you might have to stand outside and shout your order through. (www.mugiardotxoko.es; Licenciado Poza 55; pintxos from €2.50; ⏱7am-midnight Mon-Sat, noon-midnight Sun)

Yandiola
CONTEMPORARY BASQUE €€€

Inside the Azkuna Zentroa (Alhóndiga) building (see 4 Map p42, D4), Bilbao's pride and joy, is this outstanding

Q Local Life

Café Iruña

Overlooking a pretty park just off the main shopping street, **Café Iruña** (Map p42, G3; cnr Calles de Colón de Larreátegui & Berástegui; ⏱7am-1am Mon-Thu, 7am-2am Fri, 9am-1am Sat, noon-1am Sun), with its fabulously ornate Moorish style and a century of gossip written into the walls, is the perfect place to indulge in a bit of people-watching. It works equally well for coffee, lunch or an evening drink. Don't miss the delicious *pinchos morunos* (spicy kebabs).

restaurant where chef Ricardo Perez prepares modern Basque and Spanish fare that is as highly touted as the building itself. It's quite popular with business groups. The complex houses some cheaper eating options as well. (📞944 13 36 36; www.yandiola.com; Plaza Alhóndiga 4; menús €49.50-65, mains €23-25; ⏱1-4pm & 8.30-11pm)

Larruzz Bilbao
MEDITERRANEAN €€

19 Map p42, F2

Set on the banks of the Nervión, this incredibly popular restaurant (book ahead) has a polished business exterior and a stone-cottage country interior. Its real speciality is paella, but it also serves various meaty Mediterranean dishes. (📞944 23 08 20; www. larruzzbilbao.com; Calle Uribitarte 24; menú del día €15.50, menús €29-45, mains €12-17; ⏱noon-midnight)

El Huevo Frito
PINTXOS €

20 Map p42, D3

With its relaxed, casual vibe, the welcoming 'Fried Egg' is a prime spot for exceptional *pintxos*. The bar is laden with tempting offerings but it's the hot dishes that really stand out – the grilled foie gras (*foie a la plancha*) is superb. (📞944 41 22 49; Calle Maestro Garcia Rivero 1; pintxos about €3.50; ⏱9am-11pm Mon-Wed, to 1am Thu-Sat)

El Puertito
SEAFOOD €

21 Map p42, D3

On warm summer evenings, wine-sipping crowds congregate at this small bar to enjoy an oyster or six. Aficionados can choose from a chalked-up menu of French and Galician oysters, while amateurs can simply ask the knowledgeable, English-speaking staff for their recommendations. (☎944 02 62 54; Calle de Licenciado Poza 22, cnr Calle Maestro Garcia Rivero; oysters €1-3.30; ☺10am-10pm)

Drinking

Mami Lou Cupcake   CAFE

 22   Map p42, E2

This cute little cafe features 1950s decor and colourful homemade cupcakes. (www.mamiloucupcake.com; Calle Barraincua 7; ☺11am-8.30pm Mon-Sat)

Geo Cocktail Lounge   COCKTAIL BAR

 23   Map p42, D2

For a refined post-dinner cocktail, search out this lounge bar in the area south of the Guggenheim. Expect subdued lighting, low-key tunes and expertly crafted cocktails. (☎944 66 84 42; Calle Maximo Aguirre 12; ☺3pm-1.30am Tue-Sun)

Cotton Club   CLUB

 24   Map p42, C4

A historic Bilbao nightspot, the Cotton Club draws a mixed crowd to its DJ-stoked nights and regular gigs – mainly blues, jazz and rock. It's a tiny place so prepare to get up close with your fellow revellers. (☎944 10 49 51; www.cottonclubbilbao.es; Calle de Gregorio

Local Life

Deusto

Over the river from the Museo Guggenheim, and accessible via the Pedro Arrupe footbridge, the **Universidad de Deusto** (University of Deusto; www.deusto.es; Avenida de las Universidades 24) dominates the northern riverfront. This landmark building, initially one of Bilbao's largest, was designed by architect Francisco de Cubas in 1886 to house the Jesuit Deusto university.

To the southwest of the university, Deusto is a largely residential district. But if you're in the area and fancy a bite, **Deustoarrak** (944 75 41 54; Avenida Madariaga 9; mains €10-16; 9am-1am Mon-Thu, to 2.30am Fri, 10.30-2.30am Sat, 11-1am Sun) is one of a number of eateries on the neighbourhood's central strip, Avenida Madariaga.

de la Revilla 25; 8.30pm-3am Tue & Wed, to 5am Thu, to 6.30am Fri & Sat, 7pm-1.30am Sun)

Entertainment

Kafe Antzokia   LIVE MUSIC

25 ⭐ Map p42, G3

This is the vibrant heart of contemporary Basque Bilbao, featuring international rock, blues and reggae, as well as the cream of Basque rock-pop. Weekend concerts run from 10pm to 1am, followed by DJs until 5am. During the day it's a cafe, restaurant and cultural centre all rolled into one and has frequent exciting events on. Cover charge for concerts can range from about €15 upwards. (944 24 46 25; www.kafeantzokia.com; Calle San Vicente 2)

Euskalduna Palace   LIVE MUSIC

26 ⭐ Map p42, B2

About 600m downriver from the Guggenheim is this modernist gem, built on the riverbank and designed by architects Federico Soriano and Dolores Palacios, in a style that echoes the great shipbuilding works of the 19th century. The Euskalduna is home to the Bilbao Symphony Orchestra and the Basque Symphony Orchestra, and hosts a wide array of events. (944 03 50 00; www.euskalduna.net; Avenida Abandoibarra)

Shopping

Arrese   FOOD

27 🔒 Map p42, F3

With 160 years of baking experience you'd hope the cakes at this little patisserie would taste divine, but frankly, they're even better than expected. (www.arrese.biz; Calle Lopez de Haro 24; 9am-9pm Mon-Sat, 9am-3pm & 5-9pm Sun)

Chocolates de Mendaro   FOOD

28 🔒 Map p42, D3

This old-time chocolate shop created its first chocolate treats way back in

ARKAITZ MORALES/GETTY IMAGES ©

Euskalduna Palace (Palacio Euskalduna Conference and Performing Arts Centre)

1850 and is hands down the best place to ruin a diet in Bilbao. (www.chocolatesdemendaro.com; Calle de Licenciado Poza 16; ⏲10am-2pm & 4-8pm Mon-Sat)

Astarloa   BOOKS

29 🔒 Map p42, F3

All creaking wood and leather-bound volumes, this charming antique bookshop is one for browsing as much as buying. Most of the books are in Spanish, but there are a smattering of English titles hidden away, as well as old prints and artistic postcards.

(www.libreriastarloa.com; Calle Astarloa 4; ⏲10am-2pm Mon-Sat & 4-8pm Mon-Fri)

Zubiarte   SHOPPING CENTRE

30 🔒 Map p42, C1

Overlooking the river by the Deusto bridge, this impressive brick, stone and glass shopping centre was designed by US architect Robert Stern in the early 2000s. Inside, there are around 70 shops, including many big-name clothing stores. (www. zubiarte.com; Calle Lehendakari Leizaola 2; ⏲10am-10pm)

Explore

Getxo & Portugalete

Some 14km north of Bilbao, the well-to-do coastal town of Getxo makes a rewarding excursion. Its attractive sandy beaches and sea-front promenade are highlights, but there's also a pretty fishing village to explore and plenty of wonderful restaurants. Over the Unesco-listed Puente Colgante (Vizcaya Bridge), gritty Portugalete boasts a compact medieval centre and an interesting industrial museum.

The Sights in a Day

☼ Start the day in Portugalete. Check out the Gothic **Basilica de Santa María** (p58) and learn about the area's industrial past at the **Rialia Museo de la Industría** (p59). Next, grab coffee at **ghpc** (p63) before heading over **Puente Colgante** (p58) to Getxo. Stretch your legs on the seafront **Paseo de las Grandes Villas** (p59), admiring the town's extravagant villas and **Galerías de Punta Begoña** (p60) as you go. For lunch, stop off at **Tamarises Izarra** (p61).

☼ Once you've eaten, take some time to enjoy **Playa de Ereaga** (p60) before investigating the pretty fishing village above the **Puerto Viejo** (p60). It's a steep climb up the steps, but make it and you're rewarded with a picturesque jumble of whitewashed cottages. If your legs are up for it, push on to Playa de Arrigunaga and **Punta Galea** (p61).

★ Spend the evening in the Puerto Viejo. Dine on superlative seafood at **Karola Etxea** (p60) or keep it casual at laid-back **Bar Arrantzale** (p63).

♥ Best of Getxo & Portugalete

Eating
Karola Etxea (p60)

Beaches
Playa de Ereaga (p60)

Architecture
Puente Colgante (p58)

Getting There

Ⓜ **Metro** The best way to access both Portugalete and Getxo from central Bilbao. Portugalete has its own station on line 2; Getxo is best served by Algorta (for the beach) and Areeta (for Puente Colgante), both on line 1.

🚌 **Bus** No A3151 serves Portugalete from Bilbao's Gran Vía de Don Diego Lopez de Haro; No A3414 serves Getxo, also from the Gran Vía.

E

Aiboa M

NEGURI

M Neguri

D

M Algorta

Punta Galea
(2.5km)

17

ALGORTA

Av Algorta

Av Basagoiti

14

Muelle de Ereaga

Reina Maria
Cristina

Galerías de
Punta Begoña

Lezama-
Legizamón

12

Casa Cisco

Playa de
Ereaga

8

7

Paseo Marqués de Arriluce

18

11

19

Estación de
Salvamento
Náufragos

9

Puerto
Viejo

C

Whale
Watching

10

El Abra Marina

B

500 m

0.25 miles

A

N

1

2

3

4

GETXO

Ⓜ Gobela

C Neguri

C Caja de Ahorros ✕ 13

Ⓜ Areeta

Paseo de las
Grandes Villas ◉ 6

Muelle de las Arenas Areeta

Av Zugatzarte

C Las Mercedes

✕ Mayor

LAS
ARENAS

✕ 15

Playa de
las Arenas

Monument to
Evaristo Churruca

Muelle Evaristo
Churruca

Puente
Colgante 1 ◉

✕ 20

See Enlargement

Ria del Nervión

C Maria Dia de Haro

PORTUGALETE

Av de
Carlos VII

C Gregorio Uzquiano

Ⓜ Portugalete

Ⓜ Peñota

 Ⓚ Peñota

 Ⓚ Santurtzi

C de Sotera
de la Mier

Ria del Nervión

Rialia Museo
de la Industria 5 ◉

Paseo de
la Canilla

Parque
Azeta

ⓚ Portugalete (Renfe)
Train Station

Enlargement:

Ria del Nervión

2 Plaza del
◉ Solar

Torre de
Salazar

4 ◉

C Santa Maria

3 Basilica de
◉ Santa Maria

C Santa Maria

C Don Victor Chavarri

Cantón de la Iglesia

C de Coscojales

✕ 16

0   100 m

Sights

Puente Colgante
BRIDGE

1 Map p56, C7

Designed by Alberto Palacio, a disciple of Gustave Eiffel, the Unesco World Heritage–listed Puente Colgante (also known as the Vizcaya or Bizkaia Bridge) was the world's first transporter bridge, opening in 1883. The bridge, which links the towns of Getxo and Portugalete (part of greater Bilbao), consists of a suspended platform that sends cars and passengers gliding silently over the Ría del Nervión.

You can take a lift up to the superstructure at 46m and walk across for some great views or join a guided tour

> ## Top Tip
>
> ### Tourist Information
>
> Both Getxo and Portugalete have helpful tourist offices where you can pick up maps and local information. The Portugalete **office** (☏944 72 93 14; www.portugalete.com; Paseo de la Canilla; ☺10am-2pm daily & 4-6pm Mon-Fri winter, 10am-3pm & 4-7pm daily summer) occupies a distinctive blue-and-yellow building on the waterfront near Plaza del Solar, while Getxo's **main office** (☏944 91 08 00; www.getxo.eus/tourism; ☺9.30am-2.30pm & 4-7pm, closed Sun afternoon Oct-May) is on Playa de Ereaga. Getxo also has an **information point** (☏615 756290; ☺10.30am-2.30pm & 4-8pm Easter-Oct) by Puente Colgante.

for a more detailed look. (www.puente -colgante.com; per person €0.35, walkway €9, guided tours €45; ☺5am-10pm, walkway 10am-7pm Nov-Mar, 10am-8pm Mon-Thu, to 9pm Fri Apr-Oct; Ⓜ Areeta, Portugalete)

Plaza del Solar
PLAZA

2 Map p56, E7

At the foot of Portugalete's medieval centre, this cobbled square makes for a fine photo with its handsome 19th-century buildings and august monument to Victor de Chavarri, an important local industrialist. Nearby, an ornate bandstand provides the stage for regular Sunday performances by the local brass band.

Basilica de Santa María
BASILICA

3 Map p56, E8

Portugalete's impressive basilica (1580) stands atop an earlier 14th-century church that originally marked the town's highest point. A striking structure, it's largely Gothic with flying buttresses and austere sandstone walls; the bell tower was a later 18th-century addition. Inside, the carved wood altarpiece is a highlight. (Cantón de la Iglesia; ☺10.30am-1pm & 4.30-8pm mid-Jun–mid-Sep, services only rest of year)

Torre de Salazar
TOWER

4 Map p56, E8

This stubby tower was originally part of a defensive complex built by the local Salazar family during a period of baronial fighting in the 15th century.

Puente Colgante

It subsequently served as the family's fortified residence, and today houses a museum chronicling the Salazar's colourful history. (Travesía Lope Garcia de Salazar; ⏰5.30-8.30pm Tue-Fri, 11am-2pm & 5.30-8.30pm Sat, 11am-2pm Sun)

Rialia Museo de la Industría
MUSEUM

 5 ◉ Map p56, C8

Learn about Portugalete's industrial history at this small waterfront museum. Exhibits, which include paintings and machinery parts, chart the town's development and the effect early industrialisation had on the area's landscape and social make-up. (✏944 72 43 84; www.rialia.net; Paseo de la Canilla; admission €2; ⏰11am-2.30pm & 3.30-6pm Tue-Fri Oct-May, 11am-2.30pm & 5-7pm Tue-Fri Jun-Sep, 11am-2pm Sat & Sun year-round)

Paseo de las Grandes Villas
AREA

 6 ◉ Map p56, C5

The Paseo is the unofficial name given to Getxo's seafront – made up of Muelle de las Arenas Areeta and Paseo Marques e Arriluce. The 'Villas' part of the name is a reference to the extravagant mansions that pepper the route, many of which date to the town's heyday in the early 20th century. Two to look out for are the Nordic-style **Casa Cisco** (Map p56, D4) and castle-like **Lezama-Legizamón** (Map p56, D3).

Galerías de Punta Begoña
LANDMARK

7 Map p56, C3

This massive brown structure was built in 1919 as a protective sea wall. It's an impressive sight, complete with columns and a balustraded terrace, and while it's rarely open to the public, guided visits are sometimes laid on – it depends on the state of the ongoing restoration; check with the tourist office. Opposite the gallery is Bilbao's first lighthouse, the Estacíon de Salvamento de Náufragos; it now houses a Red Cross station. (Muelle de Ereaga)

Playa de Ereaga
BEACH

8 Map p56, C2

Getxo's principal summer attraction is the Playa de Ereaga, the long sandy beach that runs between the Galerías de Punta Begoña and Puerto Viejo. A better beach, Playa de Arrigunaga, lies to the north of the town centre, sandwiched between Punta Galea and a bushy hill.

Top Tip
Ereaga Lift
Save yourself legwork by taking the lift to Playa de Ereaga from Reina Maria Cristina just off Avenida Algorta. It costs €0.20 and runs from 9am to 11pm Sunday through Thursday, and to half past midnight on Fridays and Saturdays.

Puerto Viejo
AREA

9 Map p56, C1

Getxo's old port sits at the northern end of Playa de Ereaga. There's not much to see there now, but go up the steps and you emerge into a charming enclave of fishermen's cottages and alleyways.

Whale-Watching
WILDLIFE WATCHING

10 Map p56, C3

Operating out of El Abra marina, Náutica Potxolo runs day-long whale-watching cruises each Saturday and Sunday from late July to November. Sightings are not guaranteed but with 27 whale species in the Bay of Biscay, you stand a reasonable chance. You'll need to bring your own food. (☎688 657042; www.avistamientodecetaceos.com; Puerto Deportivo de Getxo; per person €90)

Eating

Karola Etxea
BASQUE €€€

11 Map p56, C1

The cosy, wood-beamed dining room of this Puerto Viejo restaurant, quaintly housed in a picture-perfect white cottage, sets the stage for quality Basque food. The onus is on fresh seafood – prawns, cod, hake – but there's also a select choice of steak and meat dishes. To sample the wares for a snip of the regular price, try the €18 fixed-price menu served Monday through Friday. (☎944 60 08 68; www.karolaetxea.net; Calle Aretxondo 22, Getxo; mains €20-24; ⊙1-4pm & 9-11pm)

Tamarises Izarra
BASQUE €€€

12 Map p56, D2

At this smart beachside place, you can dine on innovative Basque cuisine in the formal upstairs restaurant or dig into a bargain €10 *menú* on the sunny sea-facing terrace. Orchestrating things in the kitchen is Chef Javier Izarra, whose brand of creative contemporary cuisine has earned him plaudits from locals and visitors alike. (📞944 91 00 05; www.tamarisesizarra.com; Muelle de Ereaga 4, Getxo; tasting menu €45, mains €16-26; ⏱1-4pm & 8pm-midnight)

Tudelilla Gure Etxea
BASQUE €€

13 Map p56, D6

This traditional restaurant hidden away on a backstreet in Las Arenas' pedestrianised centre is a local favourite. And with its outdoor tables, inviting woody interior and choice of locally caught fish and *solomillo* (sirloin) steaks, it hits the mark perfectly. A bargain €10 daily *menú* is served Monday through Friday. (📞944 64 08 82; Calle Caja de Ahorros 12, Getxo; mains €10-18; ⏱1-4pm & 9-11pm, closed Sun & Mon evening)

Satistegi
SEAFOOD €€

14 Map p56, D1

Revel in sweeping sea views and excellent seafood at this modish bar-restaurant in Getxo's Algorta district. Behind its handsome facade, the sleek interior, all blond wood, high tables and a transparent fish tank, is a relaxed spot to linger over a bottle of wine and platters of grilled prawns. (📞944 36 28

Punta Galea

Jutting into the sea north of Playa de Arrigunaga, the promontory of Punta Galea offers wonderful walking. The area, which is geologically unique thanks to its exposed rock strata, boasts superb sea views, surfing at Playa de Gorrondatxe Aizkorri, the remains of an 18th-century defensive fort and a landmark windmill.

58; Avenida Basagoiti 51, Getxo; pintxos €1.50-3.50, mains €7.50-18.50; ⏱8am-midnight Mon-Fri, 9am-1am Sat & Sun)

La Kazuela
BASQUE €€

15 Map p56, C6

A friendly, modern bar-restaurant in Getxo's lively Las Arenas district. If you don't fancy a sit-down meal, try the *pintxos* – the salmon and tuna creations are excellent – while for something more substantial, go for a *racione* of Cantabrian anchovies. (📞946 08 06 02; www.lakazuela.com; Calle Mayor 17, Getxo; daily menú €11.90, mains €9-13; ⏱7am-midnight Mon-Fri, 8am-1am Sat & Sun)

Restaurante Torre de Salazar
BASQUE €€

Dine while admiring views over the Puente Colgante at this glass-walled restaurant in the Torre de Salazar (see 4 ⊙ Map p56, E8). There are various menus to choose from, each offering traditional Basque surf and turf and excellent value for money. (📞644 070534;

Understand

A Basque History Lesson

No one quite knows where the Basque people came from (they have no migration myth in their oral history), but their presence here is believed to predate even the earliest known migrations. The Romans left the hilly Basque Country more or less to itself, but the expansionist Castilian crown gained sovereignty over Basque territories during the Middle Ages (1000–1450), although with considerable difficulty; Navarra constituted a separate kingdom until 1512. Even when they came within the Castilian orbit, Navarra and the three other Basque provinces (Guipúzcoa, Vizcaya and Álava) extracted broad autonomy arrangements, known as the *fueros* (the ancient laws of the Basques).

After the Second Carlist War in 1876, all provinces except Navarra were stripped of their coveted *fueros*, thereby fuelling nascent Basque nationalism. Yet, although the Partido Nacionalista Vasco (PNV; Basque Nationalist Party) was established in 1894, support was never uniform as all Basque provinces included a considerable Castilian contingent.

When the Republican government in Madrid proposed the possibility of home rule (self-government) to the Basques in 1936, both Guipúzcoa and Vizcaya took up the offer. When the Spanish Civil War erupted, conservative rural Navarra and Álava supported Franco, while Vizcaya and Guipúzcoa sided with the Republicans, a decision they paid a high price for in the four decades that followed.

It was during the Franco days that Euskadi Ta Askatasuna (ETA; Basque Homeland and Freedom) was first born. It was originally set up to fight against the Franco regime, which suppressed the Basques by banning the language and almost all forms of Basque culture. After the death of Franco, ETA called for nothing less than total independence and continued its bloody fight against the Spanish government until, in October 2011, the group announced a 'definitive cessation of its armed activity'. It's a status that still stands.

www.torredesalazar.es; Travesía Lope Garcia de Salazar, Portugalete; fixed-price menus €13-35; ⏱1.30-4pm Tue-Thu, 1-4pm & 8.30-11pm Fri & Sat, 1-4.30pm Sun)

Patxin BASQUE €€

16 🍴 Map p56, D8

A reliable choice in Portugalete's historic centre, this modest restaurant serves decent portions of no-nonsense regional fare such as *bacalao al pil-pil* (salted cod with garlic sauce) and grilled squid. The restaurant is upstairs from the street-level bar. (☎944 96 11 85; www.restaurantepatxin.com; Calle de Coscojales 17, Portugalete; daily menú €12.80, mains €16-23; ⏱1-4pm & 8.30-10.30pm Mon-Thu, 1-4pm & 9.30-11.30pm Fri & Sat, 2-4pm Sun)

Cubita Aixerrota SEAFOOD €€€

17 🍴 Map p56, D1

Built into the windmill that overlooks Playa de Arrigunaga, this much-lauded restaurant specialises in top-of-the-line seafood. Wine buffs will also enjoy the formidable list of largely Spanish and French labels. (☎944 91 17 00; www.restaurantecubita.com; Carretera de Galea 30, Getxo; mains €20-30; ⏱1.30-4pm & 8.30pm-midnight, closed Wed & Sun evening)

Drinking

Bar Arrantzale BAR

18 🍺 Map p56, C1

With its delightful shaded terrace and charming setting in Getxo's white-washed Puerto Viejo, this laid-back bar is a top spot to slow down over a

 Top Tip

Water Sports

Getxo is a hot spot for water sports with everything from sailing and surfing to canoeing, diving and fly-boarding. For information on these and other activities contact **Getxo-port** (☎639 137109; www.getxoport.com; Puerto Deportivo de Getxo).

cool beer and nibble on *pintxos*. The *morcillas* (blood sausages) are wonderful. (www.arrantzale.com; Portu Zaharra 3, Getxo; ⏱noon-11pm)

Portu Zaharra Bar PUB

19 🍺 Map p56, C1

Housed in a traditional white-and-green cottage by the steps at Getxo's Puerto Viejo, this is a prime spot for a chilled drink. Park yourself on the steps and enjoy sea views while sampling the local tipple of choice, *txakoli* (a dry white wine). (Portu Zaharra 35, Getxo; ⏱6-11pm Mon, 10am-11pm Tue-Thu, to midnight Sat, to 10.30pm Sun)

ghpc BAR

20 🍺 Map p56, C7

Grab a drink and take a seat on the terrace bar of the Gran Hotel Puente Colgante. You'll be perfectly positioned to admire views of the famous bridge and watch the world stroll past on the waterfront promenade. *Pintxos* and full meals are also available. (María Dia de Haro 2, Portugalete; ⏱8am-11pm Mon-Thu & Sun, 9am-midnight Fri & Sat)

Top Sights
Guernica

Getting There

🚆 **Train** Take an ET/FV train from Bilbao's Atxuri train station (€2.85, one hour, every 30 minutes).

🚗 **Car** Guernica is just off the A8 motorway in the direction of San Sebastián.

A symbol of the violence of the 20th century, the tragedy of Guernica (Basque: Gernika) is most famously portrayed in Picasso's work of the same name. A Basque cultural centre and bastion of anti-Franco sentiment, it was here that Hitler joined forces with the Spanish general to test his new saturation bombing tactics. On 26 April 1937, a market day, hundreds of civilians were killed as Condor Legion warplanes bombarded Guernica for two hours, utterly destroying the town and ultimately demoralising the Republican resistance.

Tree of Guernica

Don't Miss

Museo de la Paz de Gernika

Guernica's seminal experience is a visit to the **Museo de la Paz de Gernika** (Guernica Peace Museum; www.peacemuseumguernica.org; Plaza Foru 1; adult/child €5/3; ☉10am-7pm Tue-Sat, 10am-2pm Sun Mar-Sep, shorter hours rest of year), where audiovisual displays reveal the horror of war. A couple of blocks north, on Calle Allende Salazar, is a ceramic-tile version of Picasso's *Guernica*. The actual painting is in Madrid's Centro de Arte Reina Sofía.

Euskal Herriko Museoa

Housed in the beautiful 18th-century Palacio de Montefuerte, the **Euskal Herriko Museoa** (Calle Allende Salazar; adult/child €3/1.50; ☉10am-2pm & 4-7pm Tue-Sat, 10.30am-2.30pm Sun) contains a comprehensive exhibition on Basque history and culture, with old maps, engravings and a range of other documents and portraits.

Parque de los Pueblos de Europa

The Parque de los Pueblos de Europa contains a couple of typically curvaceous sculptures by Henry Moore and other works by Basque sculptor Eduardo Chillida. The park leads to the attractive **Casa de Juntas**, where the provincial government has met since 1979. Nearby is the *Tree of Guernica*, under which the Basque parliament met from medieval times to 1876.

Nearby: Cuevas de Santimamiñe

The walls of this **cave system** (☎944 65 16 57; www.santimamine.com; adult/child €5/3; ☉10am-5.30pm Apr-Oct, 10am-1pm Tue-Sun Nov-Mar), northeast of Guernica, are decorated with Neolithic paintings depicting bison, horses and rhinos. Only reproductions are on display, however. Also near Guernica is Agustín Ibarrola's painted forest and a bird reserve.

☑ Top Tips

▶ Accommodation in Guernica is pretty unremarkable (though there are nicer places to stay in the vicinity), so most people just visit on a day trip from Bilbao.

▶ If you have your own car take the coastal road from Bilbao – it's slow but scenic.

✗ Take a Break

There are plenty of bars in Guernica serving high quality *pintxos* and meals. Even if it doesn't look like much from the outside, locals will tell you that **Zallo-Barri** (☎946 25 18 00; Calle Juan Calzada 79; mains €18; ☉noon-3.30pm Sun-Thu, noon-3.30pm & 8-11pm Fri & Sat) is the best place in town for quality Basque cooking.

Top Sights
Central Basque Coast

Getting There

🚗 **Car** Hiring a car is easiest, but it's a slow road and summer parking in beach towns can be difficult.

🚉 **Train** Euskotren (www.euskotren.eus) operates frequent trains to many of the coastal towns.

The coastal road from Bilbao to San Sebastián is a glorious journey past spectacular seascapes, with cove after cove stretching west and verdant fields suddenly ending where cliffs plunge into the sea. Highlights include quaint Elantxobe, the seafood heaven of Getaria and the got-it-all town of Lekeitio.

San Juan de Gaztelugatxe

Don't Miss

San Juan de Gaztelugatxe

Attached to the mainland by a short causeway, this rocky isle is topped by the hermitage of **San Juan de Gaztelugatxe** (admission free). The island is named after St John the Baptist; local tradition holds that he visited the island and that his footprint is still visible near the top of the 200-odd steps that lead up to the hermitage.

Bermeo

Although the tough fishing port of Bermeo has no beaches, it's an enjoyable place to while away a few hours watching boats in the harbour and checking out the colourful old town streets that work their way up the hill. There are some worthwhile *pintxo* bars located around the main square.

Mundaka

Regarded as the home of the best wave in Europe, Mundaka is a legend for surfers across the world, but this little beach town is also popular with locals looking for an escape from Bilbao. Fantastic for experienced surfers, the wave at Mundaka only breaks on big swells, but when it's on it makes for a memorable show.

Urdaibai Biosphere Reserve & Bird Center

The Urdaibai estuary snakes north of Guernica to kiss the sea at Mundaka. Covering around 220 sq km of constantly evolving water flows, mud banks, marshes and forests, this is a very important wetland habitat and particularly well regarded for its bird life. The impressive **Urdaibai Bird Center** (☏699 839202; www.birdcenter. org; ⏰9.30am-2pm Tue-Sun), close to the village

☑ Top Tips

▶ If you want to overnight, *casas rurales* (village or farmstead accommodation) and campgrounds are plentiful.

▶ In summer, book hotels in Lekeitio as far in advance as possible.

▶ Allow more time than you think you'll need to explore the coast.

✖ Take a Break

In Getaria, a town renowned for its seafood, it takes something special to stand out. Michelin-starred **Elkano** (☏943 14 00 24; www.restaurante elkano.com; Calle Herrieta 2; tasting menu €75; ⏰1-3.30pm & 8-10.30pm Wed-Mon) does just that, by being pure, simple and old-fashioned. No fancy sauces, no arty touches – just delicious grilled fish.

of Gautegiz-Arteaga, will teach you about the different feathered friends found here.

Elantxobe

The tiny hamlet of Elantxobe, with its colourful houses clasping like geckos to an almost sheer cliff face, is undeniably one of the most attractive spots along the entire coast. There's no beach here, but it's a pretty place to explore, and on hot days you can join the local children jumping into the sea from the harbour walls.

Ea

Water surrounds the gorgeous little village of Ea. Sitting at the head of a narrow estuary that could almost be mistaken for a shrunken-down version of a Norwegian fjord, the colourful streets of the 16th-century village are linked by humpbacked medieval bridges. On the seaward end of the village is a sandy patch of beach.

Lekeitio

Bustling Lekeitio is gorgeous. The attractive old core is centred on the unnaturally large, late-Gothic church and a busy harbour lined with multi-coloured, half-timbered buildings – some of which house fine seafood restaurants. But for most visitors, it's the two **beaches** that are the main draw. The one just east of the river is one of the finest in the Basque Country.

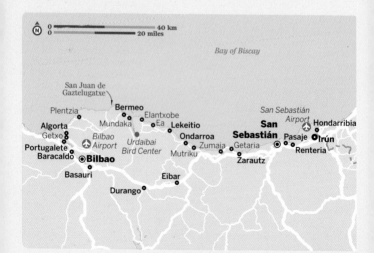

Understand
Txakoli Wine

The fishing village of Getaria is famous for its very dry, sparkling white wine known as *txakoli*. Considered an aperitif that goes well with the region's spectacular *pintxos* (tapas), *txakoli* has a low alcohol content (typically 9% to 11%) and needs to be drunk young. It doesn't really keep longer than a year. *Txakoli* is most often poured from a height (like the local cider) for a maximum bubble-to-drink ratio and good flavour.

There are several different kinds of *txakoli*; the best regarded is that grown near Getaria. This wine has a very pale yellow to greenish colour and the vines are grown on the southeast-facing slopes just inland of the town. Other *txakoli*-producing regions can be found around Bilbao and towards Vitoria.

There are several small bodegas offering tastings and tours around Getaria that are open to visitors. In all cases you need to reserve in advance. Ask at the tourist office in Getaria for booking information.

Mutriku
A fishing town through and through, Mutriku is tightly wedged between slices of steep hills. It's an attractive place of tall houses painted in blues and greens and steps that tumble steeply downwards to the port. There's no beach, but locals leap off the harbour walls to cool off in the sea.

Getaria
The attractive medieval fishing settlement of Getaria, hometown of Juan Sebastián Elkano (arguably the first person to circumnavigate the world), is a world away from cosmopolitan San Sebastián and is a much better place to get a feel for coastal Basque culture. The old village tilts gently downhill to a baby-sized harbour and a small forested island.

Cristóbal Balenciaga Museoa
Culture vultures can get their kicks at the **Cristóbal Balenciaga Museoa** (www.cristobalbalenciagamuseoa.com; adult/child/under 9yr €10/7/free; ⊙10am-7pm Jul & Aug, shorter hr Sep-Jun). Local boy Cristóbal became one of the big names in fashion design in the 1950s and '60s and this impressive museum showcases some of his best works. It's located in Getaria.

Zarautz
Zarautz consists of a 2.5km-long soft sand beach backed by a largely modern strip of tower blocks. It's a popular resort for Spaniards, and in the summer it has a lively atmosphere with plenty of places to eat, drink and stay. The beach has some of the best surfing in the area and there are a number of surf schools.

Explore

San Sebastián Parte Vieja

It only takes a couple of minutes to stroll the length of San Sebastián's Parte Vieja (Old Quarter), but it might take half a lifetime to sample all the temptations. Every other building seems to house a bar or restaurant, each of which is in intense competition with the others to please the palate.

The Sights in a Day

☀ Start the morning by San Sebastián's fishing port watching colourful trawlers return with a fishy bounty that within hours will be artistically gracing plates throughout the city. To see fish with more life to them head next to the city's impressive **aquarium** (p74), where blennies vie with sharks for your attention.

☀ For lunch it would be wrong to feast on anything else but seafood. Either head to one of the fish restaurants lining the harbourside or stick to the aquarium's own culinary temple, **Bokado** (p83). Next, head to the hills, or rather the hill, as you climb up through pretty woodland to the summit of **Monte Urgull** (p79) for big views, a small museum and a massive statue of Christ. On your way back down, you'll run straight into the architectural marvel of the **San Telmo Museoa** (p72), a Basque cultural museum with an eclectic collection that spans everything from Vespas to the *lauburu* (Basque cross).

🌙 As evening falls, the real fun begins. It's time to wander at will through the old town, grazing on the town's legendary *pintxos* (tapas) or soaking up the atmosphere of Plaza de la Constitución (pictured left).

For a local's evening in the Parte Vieja, see p76.

 Top Sights

San Telmo Museoa (p72)

Aquarium (p74)

○ **Local Life**

Following the Pintxos Trail (p76)

💜 **Best of San Sebastián**

Eating
La Cuchara de San Telmo (p77)
A Fuego Negro (p76)
Bar Borda Berri (p77)
Bodegón Alejandro (p81)

Drinking & Nightlife
Altxerri Jazz Bar (p84)

Shopping
Pukas (p85)

Museums
San Telmo Museoa (p72)

Getting There

✈ **Foot** San Sebastián is small and with the Parte Vieja sitting pretty much at the centre, it's almost always easier and quicker to walk here from elsewhere.

Top Sights
San Telmo Museoa

Although it's one of the newest museums in the Basque Country, the San Telmo Museoa has actually been around since the 1920s. It was closed for many years, but after major renovation work it reopened in 2011. The displays range from historical artefacts to the squiggly lines of modern art, with all pieces reflecting Basque culture and society.

Map p78, D2

www.santelmomuseoa.com

Plaza Zuloaga 1

adult/student/child €6/3/free

10am-8pm Tue-Sun

Don't Miss

The Design

The Basque Country likes to provide its collections with eye-catching homes and the San Telmo Museoa is no exception. The museum has taken a 16th-century Dominican convent with a beautiful cloister and added a memorable bit of contemporary architecture, even including a vertical garden.

Temporary Exhibitions

The museum prides itself on the broad outlook of its collection, but it's in the frequently changing temporary exhibitions that such diversity becomes truly apparent. These exhibitions might focus one month on mountaineering in the Basque lands and beyond; the following month it could be all about Japanese gardens with a Basque bent.

Memory Traces

Covering the vast period from prehistory to the 18th century, the *Memory Traces* exhibition delves into Basque origins and the moment in which they first looked out to the wider world and set off by boat to explore it.

The Sert Canvases

One of the museum's proudest possessions are the Sert Canvases, located inside the church. The work, created in 1929 by José María Sert, illustrates some of the most important events in San Sebastián's history including panels on shipbuilding and the sacred oak tree of Guernica.

The Awakening of Modernity

This exhibition covers the great transformations in Basque society that took place during the 19th and 20th centuries, when lifestyles changed from rural to industrial and urban. Exhibits range from traditional farming equipment to 1960s pop culture.

IAKOV FILIMONOV/SHUTTERSTOCK ©

☑ Top Tips

▶ Labelling is in Spanish and Basque, but there are free audio guides available in other languages.

▶ The connection between pieces can be vague – get a guide (audio or otherwise) to make things clearer.

▶ There are guided tours (€3) in Spanish at 5.30pm on Saturdays.

▶ Entry is free on Tuesdays.

✗ Take a Break

La Cuchara de San Telmo (p77), arguably the best *pintxo* bar in San Sebastián's old town, is located almost next door to the museum. There's also a small in-house cafe, the Bokado San Telmo (p83).

Top Sights
Aquarium

Fear for your life as huge sharks bear down behind glass panes, or gaze in disbelief at tripped-out fluoro jellyfish. Highlights include the deep-ocean and coral-reef exhibits, and the long tunnel, around which swim monsters of the deep. The aquarium also contains an excellent maritime museum section. Allow at least 1½ hours for a visit.

👁 Map p78, A3

www.aquariumss.com

Plaza Carlos Blasco de Imaz 1

adult/child €13/6.50

🕒10am-9pm daily Jul & Aug, to 8pm Mon-Fri, to 9pm Sat & Sun Easter-Jun & Sep, varies rest of year

Don't Miss

Maritime Exhibition

Overlooked by many of the aquarium's younger visitors, the maritime exhibition takes to the high seas as it explores the Basque's long and adventurous seafaring past and reveals how they were accomplished whalers, in-demand navigators (it was a Basque who was the first person to sail around the world) and, controversially, the first Europeans to discover the Americas.

Oceanarium & Tunnel

The highlight of the aquarium for young and old alike is the giant oceanarium tank which is reached via a see-through tunnel around which swim razor-toothed sharks (including a couple of bull sharks, which aren't seen in many aquariums), graceful rays, cute turtles and various other denizens of the deep.

Tactile Tank

A big hit with children is the tactile tank where they can wet their finger tips as they try to handle blennies, prawns and more. We can't guarantee that the fish in this display enjoy the experience as much as the kids...

Baby Sharks

Towards the end of the aquarium is a tank containing slightly transparent shark eggs (dogfish, not great whites) that allow you to see the unborn sharks wriggling about.

Coral Reefs & Mangrove Swamps

Everyone enjoys the over-sized tanks of beautiful corals and butterfly-bright tropical marine fish. The mangrove swamp display with tree roots reaching into the depths reveals some of the unusual creatures that live in this harsh environment.

P. EOCHE/GETTY IMAGES ©

☑ Top Tips

▶ Last tickets are sold one hour before closing.

▶ Try to avoid visiting over Easter and on wet summer days when crowds can be overwhelming.

▶ Audio guides (€2) are worth hiring for a bit more information.

✕ Take a Break

There's no cafe within the aquarium but the harbourside around the aquarium contains a number of decent seafood restaurants including **Restaurante Mariñela** (☎943 42 13 88; www.marinela-igeldo.com; Paseo del Muelle; mains €10-18; ⏱1-4pm & 9pm-midnight Tue-Sat, 1-4pm Sun). Immediately behind the aquarium (up the steps) is Bokado (p83), which has memorable views to go with its seafood dishes.

Local Life
Following the Pintxos Trail

Many a tourist brochure likes to describe San Sebastián's Parte Vieja as containing more bars per square metre than anywhere else on earth. We have no idea how true this claim is, but we do know that there's nothing the people of San Sebastián enjoy more than strolling from bar to bar with friends, sampling one *pintxo* after another.

1 **A Fuego Negro**
Dark, theatrical and anything but traditional, **A Fuego Negro** (www.afuegonegro.com; Calle 31 de Agosto 31; pintxos from €2.50) is one of the leading designers of arty *pintxos* and everything here is a surprise: expect white rabbit cutouts popping out of *pintxos* and art easel backdrops for molecular creations. This place is young, different and worth watching.

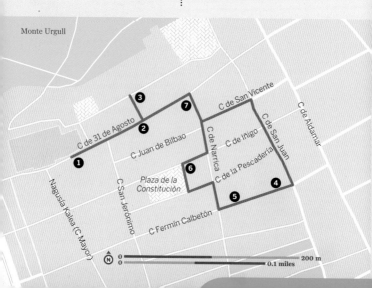

Monte Urgull

❷ Bar Martinez

Opening its doors in the 1940s, tiny **Bar Martinez** (Calle 31 de Agosto 13; pintxos from €2.50; ⏱9.30am-11pm Tue-Sun, open late Fri & Sat), with its many dusty bottles of wine, has had plenty of time to get things right, including the award-winning *morros de bacalao* (slices of cod balanced atop a piece of bread). One of the more character-laden places to stop for a bite.

❸ La Cuchara de San Telmo

La Cuchara de San Telmo (www.lacucharadesantelmo.com; Calle de 31 de Agosto 28; pintxos from €2.50; ⏱7.30-11pm Tue, noon-3.30pm & 7.30-11pm Wed-Sun) offers miniature *nueva cocina vasca* (Basque nouvelle cuisine) from a supremely creative kitchen. There aren't any *pintxos* laid out on the bar top; instead, order from the menu. Don't miss the *carrílera de ternera al vino tinto* (calf cheeks in red wine), with meat so tender it dissolves almost before it's past your lips.

❹ Bar Goiz-Argi

Gambas a la plancha (prawns cooked on a hotplate) are the house speciality of the **Bar Goiz-Argi** (Calle de Fermín Calbetón 4; pintxos from €2.50; ⏱9.30am-3.30pm & 6.30-11.30pm Wed-Sun, 9.30-3.30pm Mon). Sounds simple, we know, but never have we tasted prawns cooked quite as perfectly as this.

❺ Bar Borda Berri

The mustard-yellow **Bar Borda Berri** (Calle Fermín Calbetón 12; pintxos from €2.50; ⏱noon-midnight) is a *pintxos* bar that really stands out. The house specials are pig's ears served in garlic soup (much better than it sounds), braised veal cheeks in wine, and a mushroom and Idiazabal (a local cheese) risotto.

❻ Astelena

The *pintxos* draped across the counter of **Astelena** (Calle de Iñigo 1; pintxos from €2.50; ⏱1-4.30pm & 8-11pm Tue & Thu-Sat, 1-4.30pm Wed), tucked into the corner of Plaza de la Constitución, will have you reconsidering how full you really are. Many of them fuse Basque and Asian inspirations, but the best of all are the foie-gras-based treats. The great positioning means that prices are slightly elevated.

❼ La Viña

The bar of **La Viña** (☎943 42 74 95; www.lavinarestaurante.com; Calle de 31 de Agosto 3; pintxos from €2, mains €14-22; ⏱10.30am-5pm & 6.30pm-midnight) displays a wonderful array of fishy *pintxos* and delectable snacks, but the real highlight here is the cheesecake. Cooked daily to a special recipe and left to stand on shelves over the bar, it's creamy and flavoursome, ideal for a mid-morning snack, lunch dessert, teatime nibble or evening filler...well, any time, really.

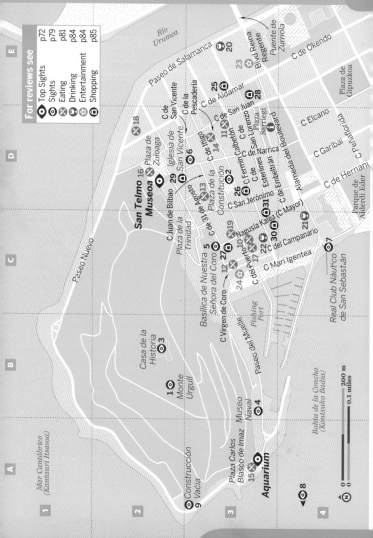

Río Urumea

Paseo de Salamanca

Mar Cantábrico (Kantauri Itsasoa)

Paseo Nuevo

San Telmo Museoa 16

Plaza de Zuloaga

Iglesia de San Vicente

C de San Vicente

C de la Pescadería

C de Íñigo

C de Aldamar

C de San Juan

Plaza de la Constitución

C Fermín Calbetón

C de San Lorenzo

Plaza Sarriegi

C de Narrica

Blvd Reina Regente

Puente de Zurriola

C de Okendo

Plaza de Gipuzkoa

C Elcano

C Garibai

C de Hernani

C Peñaflorida

Parque de Alderdi Eder

Alameda del Boulevard

C de Embeltrán

C San Jerónimo

C Esterlines

Nagusia Kalea (C Mayor)

C del Campanario

C Mari Igentea

C del Puerto

C del Muelle

C Virgen de Coro

Plaza de la Trinidad

Basílica de Nuestra Señora del Coro

C de 31 de Agosto

C Juan de Bilbao

Casa de la Historia

Monte Urgull

Fishing Port

Paseo del Muelle

Bahía de la Concha (Kontxako Badia)

Museo Naval

Plaza Carlos Blasco de Imaz

Aquarium

Construcción Vacía

Real Club Náutico de San Sebastián

200 m
0.1 miles

0
0

N

Sights

Monte Urgull
CASTLE, PARK

1 Map p78, B2

You can walk to the summit of Monte Urgull, topped by the low castle walls of the Castillo de la Mota and a grand statue of Christ, by taking a path from Plaza de Zuloaga or from behind the aquarium. The views are breathtaking and the shady parkland on the way up is a peaceful retreat from the city.

Plaza de la Constitución
PLAZA

2 Map p78, D3

One of the most attractive city squares in the Basque Country, the Plaza de la Constitución sits at the heart of the old town. The square dates from 1813 but sits on the site of an older square. It was once used as a bullring; the balconies of the fringing houses were rented to spectators.

Casa de la Historia
MUSEUM

3 Map p78, B2

Inside the grounds of the Castillo de la Mota, at the summit of Monte Urgull, is this small museum focusing on the city's history. There's a particular emphasis on the military. (www.santelmomuseoa.com/exposiciones/urgull; Monte Urgull; admission free; ⏱10am-5.30pm Wed-Sun)

Museo Naval
MUSEUM

4 Map p78, B3

This museum turns the pages of Basque seafaring and naval history. There are no English labels. (www.untzimuseoa.net; Paseo del Muelle 24; adult/student/child €3/1/free; ⏱10am-2pm & 4-7pm Tue-Sat, from 11am Sun Jul & Aug, closed Sun afternoons Sep-Jun)

Basílica de Nuestra Señora del Coro
BASILICA

5 Map p78, C3

The Parte Vieja's best-loved building is the baroque basilica of Nuestra Señora del Coro, featuring an eye-catching ornate facade depicting St Sebastián. The church was completed in 1774. The new town cathedral lies in a direct line to the south. (Calle de 31 de Agosto)

Top Tip

San Sebastián Card

The San Sebastián Card entitles users to free or reduced admission rates at many of the city's sights, free citywide transport, discounts in various shops and, with the more expensive cards, a free city tour. Cards are valid for three days (€9) and five days (€16), and are available at the tourist office.

Iglesia de San Vicente   CHURCH

6 Map p78, D3

Lording it over the Parte Vieja, this striking church is thought to be the oldest building in San Sebastián. Its origins date to the 12th century, but it was rebuilt in its current Gothic form in the early 1500s. The towering facade gives onto an echoing vaulted interior, featuring an elaborate gold altarpiece and a 19th-century French organ. Also impressive are the stained-glass rose windows. (Calle de San Vicente 3; ⊙9am-1pm & 5-8pm Mon-Fri)

Real Club Náutico de San Sebastián   HISTORIC BUILDING

7 Map p78, C4

Up by the harbour at the northeastern end of the beach, the Real Club Náutico de San Sebastián was built in 1928 in a rationalist style. Appropriately enough, it resembles a boat. (www.rcnss.com; Calle Ijentea 9)

Isla de Santa Clara   ISLAND

8 Map p78, A4

About 700m from Playa de la Concha, this island is accessible by boats (p89) that run every half-hour from the fishing port. At low tide the island gains its own tiny beach and you can climb its forested paths to a small lighthouse. There are also picnic tables and a simple cafe.

Construcción Vacía   SCULPTURE

9 Map p78, A3

At the base of Monte Urgull is Jorge Oteiza's *Construcción Vacía* (Empty Space) sculpture. Oteiza (1908–2003) was a renowned painter, sculptor and writer who was born and brought up close to San Sebastián. The work, which won an award at the Sao Paulo Biennale some fifty years ago, looks best on a dark and stormy day. (Paseo Nuevo)

Eating

With 17 Michelin stars (including three restaurants with the coveted three stars), San Sebastián is one of the culinary capitals of the planet. As if that weren't enough, the city's numerous bar tops are all weighed down by a mountain of *pintxos* that almost every Spaniard will (sometimes grudgingly) tell you are the best in the country (p76).

La Fábrica   MODERN BASQUE €€

10 🍴 Map p78, C3

The red-brick interior walls and white tablecloths lend an air of class to this restaurant, whose modern takes on Basque classics have been making waves with San Sebastián locals over the last couple of years. At just €25, the multi-dish tasting *menú* is about the best-value deal in the city. Advance reservations are essential. (📞943 98 05 81; www.restaurantelafabrica. es; Calle del Puerto 17; mains €15-20, menús from €25; ⏱12.30-4pm & 7.30-11.30pm Mon-Fri, 1-4pm & 8-11pm Sat-Sun)

Bodegón Alejandro   SEAFOOD €€

11 🍴 Map p78, D3

This oft-praised casual restaurant has a menu from which you can select such succulent treats as cod in olive

ANDER DYLAN/SHUTTERSTOCK ©

Isla de Santa Clara

oil with a crab stew, squid cooked in its own ink, or just plain-old baked lobster. (☎943 42 71 58; www.bodegonalejandro.com; Calle de Fermín Calbetón 4; menú del día from €16, mains €15-20; ☺1-3.30pm Tue & Sun, 1-3.30pm & 8.30-10.30pm Wed-Sat)

Restaurante Kokotxa

MODERN SPANISH €€€

12 Map p78, C3

This Michelin-star restaurant is hidden away down an overlooked alley in the old town, but the food rewards those who search. Most people opt for the *menú de mercado* (€60) and enjoy

---

Understand
The Gastronomic Societies of San Sebastián

Peek through the keyholes of enough Basque doors and eventually you'll come across the sight of a large room full of people seated around a table bending beneath the weight of food and drink. A restaurant? Try and enter and you'll be politely turned away. What you have just encountered is a *txoko* (Basque gastronomic society). Members of a *txoko*, who are often highly accomplished amateur chefs, meet at regular intervals to take turns cooking their own speciality for the critical consumption of the other members. The day's chef brings along all his own ingredients and, afterwards, everyone chips in their share to cover the food and a symbolic cost per attendee. As you might expect, it's often said that the best Basque food is found at a *txoko*.

A *txoko* is more than just a place to meet, though. The members are normally deeply involved in the cultural activities of a town and make up the bulk of the tamborrada drummers who parade through the streets on San Sebastián Day (20 January). Traditionally, *txoko* were exclusively male affairs, but nowadays women are normally welcome (though some remain exclusively male preserves). Women, however, are not allowed to cook – though they are allowed to do the washing up. Non-members, either male or female, are not welcome unless invited, except for on San Sebastián Day when many *txoko* open their doors to everyone.

Txoko tend to be rather conservative establishments and there are many rules governing how they are run. In the more traditional *txoko* it might be prohibited to talk about politics. During the Franco era, however, when the Basque language was banned, the *txoko* was one of the few fairly safe places where people could meet and talk – and sing – in Basque. Ultimately, the organisations helped to preserve more than just the language. Their conservatism is also said to have helped preserve certain traditional Basque recipes as well.

the flavours of the traders from the busy city market. It's closed for parts of February, June and October. (☎943 42 19 04; www.restaurantekokotxa.com; Calle del Campanario 11; mains €25-31, menús from €60; ⏱1.30-3.30pm & 8.45-11pm Tue-Sat)

Restaurante Alberto SEAFOOD €

13 Map p78, D3

A charming old seafood restaurant with a fishmonger-style window display of the day's catch. It's friendly, and the pocket-sized dining room feels like it was once someone's living room. The food is earthy (well, salty) and good, and the service swift. (☎943 42 88 84; Calle de 31 de Agosto 19; mains €12-15, menús €15; ⏱noon-4pm & 7pm-midnight Thu-Tue)

Bar Nestor BASQUE €€

14 Map p78, D3

It would be very easy to overlook this dated-looking bar, but for those in the know this place has exceptional steaks, best when enjoyed alongside grilled green peppers. It's very popular and there's very little space, so get there when it opens to ensure you get a table. (☎943 42 48 73; www.barnestor. com; Calle de la Pescadería 11; steak from €14; ⏱noon-4pm & 7pm-midnight)

Bokado SEAFOOD €€€

15 Map p78, A3

Part of the aquarium complex, stylish Bokado is all about the views. First there are the memorable panoramas over the Bahía de la Concha, and then there is the food, which looks so good

you'll be wanting to snap pictures of delicacies such as a giant prawn wave and goose barnacle brochettes! (☎943 43 18 42; www.bokadomikelsantamaria.com; Plaza Jacques Cousteau 1; menús from €42, mains €22-26; ⏱1.30-3.30pm & 9-11pm Wed-Sat, 1.30-3.30pm Sun & Tue)

Bokado San Telmo PINTXOS €

16 Map p78, D2

The San Telmo's in-house cafe is a bright change from many of the more traditional bars in San Sebastián. Expect wall-sized modern art, a canteen-like setting and *pintxos* that are as artistic as the work on display in the museum. (☎943 57 36 26; Plaza Zuloaga; pintxos €2-3; ⏱10am-8pm Tue-Sun)

La Mejíllonera SEAFOOD €

17 Map p78, C3

If you thought mussels only came with garlic sauce, come here to discover them by the thousand in all their glorious forms. Mussels not for you? Opt for the calamari and *patatas bravas* (fried potatoes with a spicy tomato and mayo sauce). We promise you won't regret it. (Calle del Puerto 15; pintxos from €2.50; ⏱11.30am-3pm & 6-11pm)

Kaskazuri SEAFOOD €€

18 Map p78, D2

Upmarket Basque seafood is all the rage in this flash restaurant, which is built on a raised platform allowing views of the former home of your dinner. It cooks up a storm with the €19 *menú del día*. (☎943 42 08 94;

www.kaskazuri.com; Paseo de Salamanca 14; menús from €19; ⏱1-3.30pm & 8.30-11pm)

Sirimiri Atari Akademy PINTXOS €

19 Map p78, C3

A bit smarter than many of the bars in the Parte Vieja, this contemporary joint dishes up a modern, jazzy vibe, artful *pintxos* and skilfully shaken cocktails. It can get very busy, so you may be tempted to sneak out and munch on the steps of the nearby basilica. Next door is its more traditional sister outfit, Atari. (☑943 44 03 14; www.sirimirigastroleku.com; Calle de Mayor 18; pintxos from €2.50; ⏱4pm-1.30am Mon, Wed & Thu, to 3am Fri, noon-late Sat & Sun)

Drinking

Be Bop BAR, CLUB

20 Map p78, E3

This long-standing and snazzy jazz bar has occasional live performances. It attracts a slightly older crowd than some of the old-town bars and on weekends it jams till dawn. (www.barbebop.com; Paseo de Salamanca 3; ⏱8pm-3am)

Dioni's GAY

21 Map p78, C4

More of a spot for black coffee in the early hours, this relaxed, gay-friendly place has a glam 1980s cocktail-bar ambience and has attracted more than its fair share of Hollywood glitz, including John Travolta and Mel Gibson. (www.dionisbar.com; Calle Ijentea 2; ⏱3pm-2.30am Mon-Thu & Sun, 3pm-3.30am Fri & Sat)

Gu COCKTAIL BAR

This modish cocktail bar has recently taken up residence in the Real Club Náutico de San Sebastián (see 7 Map p78, C4). With its slick design and glorious beach views, it sets a memorable stage for late-night cocktails and DJ sets. (☑620 898958; www.gusansebastian.com; Ijentea 9; ⏱6pm-5am Sun-Thu, to 6.30am Fri, 5pm-6.30am Sat)

Côte Bar COCKTAIL BAR

22 Map p78, C3

Once the *pintxos* bars have battened down the hatches for the night, search out this low-key cocktail bar to see in the small hours. It's a smart, good-looking place where you can sip on classic cocktails and superlative G&Ts. (☑943 43 32 10; www.coteculture.com, Calle de Fermín Calbertón 4; ⏱5pm-3am)

Entertainment

Altxerri Jazz Bar LIVE MUSIC

23 Map p78, E3

This jazz and blues temple has regular live gigs by local and international stars. Jamming sessions take over on nights with no gig; there's also an in-house art gallery. (www.altxerri.eu; Blvd Reina Regente 2; ⏱4pm-3am)

Etxekalte JAZZ

24 Map p78, C3

A late-night haunt near the harbour, which moves to dance music and grooves to jazz. There's a guest DJ most weeks. (www.etxekalte.com; Calle Mari Igentea; ⏰6pm-4am Tue-Thu & Sun, 6pm-5am Fri & Sat)

Shopping

Aitor Lasa   FOOD

25 🔒 Map p78, E3

This high-quality deli is the place to stock up on ingredients for a gourmet picnic you'll never forget. It specialises in cheeses, mushrooms and seasonal products. (www.aitorlasa.com; Calle de Aldamar 12)

Elkar   BOOKS

26 🔒 Map p78, D3

For a huge range of travel books and guides, maps and hiking books in English, Spanish and French, try this specialist travel bookshop. Almost opposite is a bigger mainstream **branch** (Calle de Fermin Calbetón 21) featuring Spanish- and Basque-language books. (www.elkar.eus; Calle de Fermín Calbetón 30; ⏰10am-2pm & 4.30-8pm Mon-Sat)

Kukuxumusu   CLOTHING

27 🔒 Map p78, C3

The funkiest and best-known Basque clothing label has a whole wardrobe of original T-shirts and other clothing awaiting you here. (Nagusía Kalea 15; ⏰10.30am-2.15pm & 4.30-8.15pm Mon-Tue, 10.30am-8.30pm Wed-Sat, 11am-3pm & 4-8pm Sun)

Mercado de la Bretxa   MARKET

28 🔒 Map p78, E3

On the east side of the Parte Vieja, this is where every chef in the old town comes to get the freshest produce. It's a good place to stock up on picnic supplies and a worthwhile sight in its own right. (Alameda del Boulevard)

Nómada   ARTS & CRAFTS

29 🔒 Map p78, D2

For something really special, check out the exquisite carpets, bags and other artefacts here, all ethically sourced by the proprietors. There are also superb artworks on fabric by Basque painters. (📞943 42 61 52; www.nomada.biz; Calle de 31 de Agosto 24)

Pukas   SPORTS

30 🔒 Map p78, C3

Pukas is a historic name in San Sebastián's surfing circles, running a surf school near Zurriola beach and a number of shops across town. As well as an array of boards, you can browse the full range of beach fashions. (📞943 42 72 28; www.pukasssurf.com; Calle Mayor 5; ⏰10am-8pm Mon-Sat, noon-2.30pm & 5.30-8pm Sun)

Euskal Linge   HANDICRAFTS

31 🔒 Map p78, C3

This shop specialises in local Basque linens woven into towels, tablecloths, aprons, bags and dressing gowns. Designs feature bright, bold colours; quality is high. (📞943 10 20 28; www.euskal-linge.com; Calle Mayor 8; ⏰10am-7pm)

Explore

San Sebastián New Town & Monte Igueldo

Elegant and gracious, San Sebastián's new town, or Centro Román-tico, has a different feel than the old city. Here the streets are wide, straight and lined by stately buildings and glam boutiques. It's a fab area for strolling about and admiring the belle époque architecture. Further west is the upmarket neighbourhood of Ondarreta and fun-filled Monte Igueldo.

The Sights in a Day

☼ Start the day at the **Catedral del Buen Pastor de San Sebastián** (p95), with its cloud-scraping tower. From here, head to the river stopping at **Chocolates de Mendaro** (p101) to buy a treat or two. Follow the river down past the **Hotel Maria Cristina** (p95) and then across to the **Plaza de Gipuzkoa** (p95) with its flowers and duck pond. After you've fed the ducks, stroll down to the **Ayuntamiento** (p94), which is one of the city's finest examples of belle époque architecture. Whether it's street performers, balloon sellers or political demonstrations, there's always something interesting going on in the adjacent **Parque de Alderdi de Eider** (p94).

☼ Enjoy a long lunch of refined Basque dishes at **Lanziego** (p98) and then walk all the way to Ondarreta to take the **funicular railway** (p91) up to the summit of **Monte Igueldo** (p90; pictured), where you'll find romantic views and tacky fairground rides.

☽ After the sun sets, head for a stiff drink at the fabulous **Museo del Whisky** (p99).

👁 Top Sights

Playa de la Concha (p88)

Monte Igueldo (p90)

🖤 Best of San Sebastián

Eating
Lanziego (p98)

Antonio Bar (p97)

Kata 4 (p98)

Drinking & Nightlife
Museo del Whisky (p99)

Koh Tao (p99)

Botanika (p100)

Architecture
Ayuntamiento (p94)

Puente de Maria Cristina (p97)

Shopping
San Sebastián Food Gourmet Shop (p101)

For Kids
Monte Igueldo (p90)

Playa de Ondarreta (p94)

Isla de Santa Clara (p89)

Getting There

➌ Foot Getting around San Sebastián's new town is best done on foot. It's about a 15-minute walk to the central part of Playa de la Concha.

Top Sights
Playa de la Concha

Fulfilling almost every idea of what a perfect city beach should be like, Playa de la Concha (and its westerly extension, Playa de Ondarreta) is framed by the Parte Vieja, beautiful parks and flowery belle époque buildings. Few people would argue its status as one of the best city beaches in Europe. Throughout the long summer months a fiesta atmosphere prevails, with thousands of tanned and toned bodies spread across the sand. Its sheltered position means the swimming is almost always safe.

👁 Map p92, E4

Don't Miss

The Beach & Paseo de la Concha

Playa de la Concha is a wide half-moon-shaped bay of soft sand, lapping waves, stunning views and a buzzing beach scene. The promenade that curves along the 1.3km-long beach makes for a lovely stroll. Lined by an ornamental wrought-iron balustrade, it's a favourite with joggers and strollers, particularly in the early evening when everyone turns out to enjoy the bracing sea air and soft summer light.

Historic Buildings

Overlooking the north of the beach, the Palacio Miramar was the summer villa of Marie Cristina, a beach-loving 19th-century royal. Further around, La Perla spa and restaurant complex is a local landmark, an ornate pavilion occupying what was once the royal bathing house. Its saltwater spas can now be enjoyed by everyone at the **Perla Thalasso Sports Centre** (☎943 45 88 56; www.la-perla.net; Paseo la Concha; thalasso treatment from €26.50).

Beachfront Partying

The Playa hosts a number of cafes and nightlife hot spots, such as Café de la Concha. For late-night dancing, the historic Bataplan Disco (p100) overlooking the sand is the place to go.

Isla de Santa Clara

About 700m from Playa de la Concha, this island is accessible by **boat** (www.motorasdelaisla.com; Lasta Plaza s/n; normal boat €4, glass-bottom boat €6; ⊙10am–8pm Jun-Sep) or by swimming (it's a long round-trip swim, though). At low tide the island gains its own tiny beach and you can climb its forested paths to a small lighthouse.

☑ Top Tips

▶ The swim out to Isla de Santa Clara is tempting, but it's further than it looks. Go from Playa de Ondarreta instead. It's closer and there are rest platforms on the way.

▶ There's normally little in the way of surf here, but even so obey the lifeguards because conditions change fast.

▶ Parking close to the beach is very difficult in the summer.

✕ Take a Break

There are lots of places to grab an ice cream or snack around the beach. Built into the pavilions that back the beach is the art deco **Café de la Concha** (☎943 47 36 00; www.cafedelaconcha. com; Paseo de la Concha 10; menús from €15, mains from €12), which has a fair-priced lunch menu and out-of-this-world views. For something more upmarket, try nearby Lanziego (p98).

Top Sights
Monte Igueldo

At the far western end of the Bahía de la Concha is the fun-filled Monte Igueldo. Attractions include a funicular railway to the summit and a funfair. While this might sound like child's play, the views from the top are like nectar to lovers of sunsets. Clifftop coastal walks also provide inspiration for hikers to make the trip.

👁 Map p92, A2

www.monteigueldo.es

🕙10am-10pm Jun-Sep, shorter hours rest of year

It's a 40-minute walk from the city centre to the base of Monte Igueldo, or take bus 16 (at Plaza de Gipuzkoa or Plaza de Buen Pastor)

Don't Miss

The Views

The views from the summit of Monte Igueldo will make you feel like a circling hawk staring over the vast panorama of the Bahía de la Concha and the surrounding coastline and mountains.

Funicular Railway

The **funicular railway** (www.monteigueldo.es; Plaza del Funicular; return adult/child €3.15/2.35; ⏰ roughly 10am-9pm Jun-Aug, shorter hours rest of year) has been clattering up the side of Monte Igueldo since the 1920s, allowing you to enjoy old-world transport. It's the best option for accessing the glorious views from the top of the hill.

Parque de Atracciones

At the **funfair** (www.monteigueldo.es; admission €2.20; ⏰ 11.15am-2pm & 4-8pm Mon-Fri, until 8.30pm Sat & Sun Jul-Sep, shorter hours rest of year) atop Monte Igueldo, individual attractions include roller coasters, boat rides, carousels and pony rides. Each ride costs between €1 and €2.50.

Sunset

When the weather gods are smiling, Monte Igueldo is a fine place to be at sunset: watch as the orange sun drops into the ocean and the lighthouse adds its own light show.

Coastal Walks

You can follow a coastal footpath westwards along the sheer cliffs and small coves for as far as you care to walk.

Torreón de Monte Igueldo

The striking Torreón de Monte Igueldo (Tower of Monte Igueldo) is a fortified 16th-century lighthouse. It no longer works (there's a new lighthouse nearby) but it offers a great vantage point.

JORGE TUTOR/ALAMY ©

☑ Top Tips

▶ Weekends, when local families come with children, might be the busiest time to visit, but it's also the most festive.

▶ Bring your beach things and stop for a dip in the calm waters of Playa de Ondarreta on the way back to the city centre.

▶ Evening visits reward with great lighthouse views.

✕ Take a Break

There are various cheap and cheerful snack bars at the top of Monte Igueldo, but our advice is bring a picnic and enjoy the view. If you prefer something more formal, try the seafood and seaviews of **Branka** (☎ 943 31 70 96; www. branka-tenis.com; Paseo Eduardo Chillida 13; mains €12-18, tasting menu €36; ⏰ 1.30-4pm & 8pm-midnight Mon-Sat), which is at the base of the hill close to the funicular station.

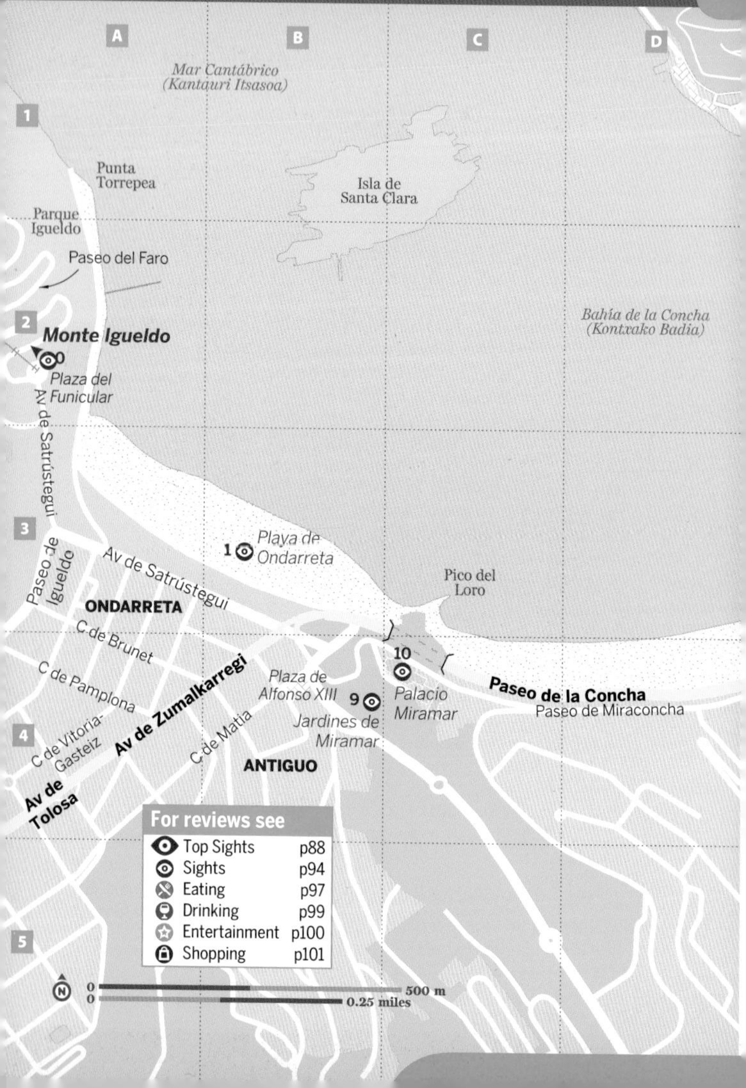

A   B   C   D

1

Mar Cantábrico
(Kantauri Itsasoa)

Punta
Torrepea

Isla de
Santa Clara

Parque
Igueldo

Paseo del Faro

2 **Monte Igueldo**

Bahía de la Concha
(Kontxako Badia)

Plaza del
Funicular

Paseo de Satrústegui

3

Paseo de Igueldo

Av de Satrústegui

Playa de
1 ⊙ Ondarreta

Pico del
Loro

ONDARRETA

C de Brunet

C de Pamplona

Av de Zumalkarregi

Plaza de
Alfonso XIII

10
⊙

9 ⊙ Palacio
Miramar

Paseo de la Concha

C de Vitoria-
Gasteiz

C de Matía

Jardines de
Miramar

Paseo de Miraconcha

**Av de
Tolosa**

ANTIGUO

For reviews see	
⊙ Top Sights	p88
⊙ Sights	p94
⊗ Eating	p97
⊕ Drinking	p99
⊛ Entertainment	p100
🔒 Shopping	p101

5

Ⓝ 0 _____ 500 m
   0 _____ 0.25 miles

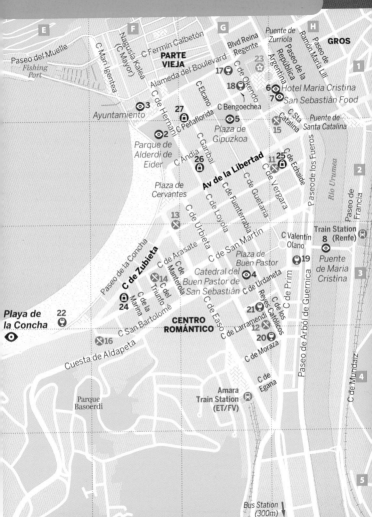

E

F

G

H

Paseo del Muelle

Fishing
Port

Nagusia Kalea
(C Mayor)

C Marijentea

C Fermín Calbetón

PARTE
VIEJA

Alameda del Boulevard

Blvd Reina
Regente

Puente de
Zurriola

Paseo de
Ramón María Lili

GROS

1

23

17

C de Okendo

18

C Elcano

C de Hernani

3

Ayuntamiento

27

C Peñaflorida

C Bengoechea

C de la República
Argentina

Paseo de la
Argentina

6 Hotel Maria Cristina
7 San Sebastián Food

2

Plaza de
Gipuzkoa

C Sta
Catalina

15

Puente de
Santa Catalina

Parque de
Alderdi de
Eider

C de Garibai

C Andia

26

Av de la Libertad

11 25 C de Echaide

C de Vergara

Paseo de los Fueros

Río Urumea

Paseo de
Francia

2

Plaza de
Cervantes

C de Urbieta

13

C de Loyola

C de Fuenterrabia

C de Guetaria

C de San Martín

C Valentín
Olano

Train Station
8 (Renfe)

Puente
de Maria
Cristina

3

Paseo de la Concha

C de Zubieta

C de Arasate

C del Triunfo

C de la Marina

C de Mantería

14

24

Catedral del
Buen Pastor de
San Sebastián

4

Plaza de
Buen Pastor

C de Urdaneta

C de Easo

19

C de Prim

C de los
Reyes Católicos

Paseo de Árbol de Guernica

Playa de
la Concha

22

C San Bartolomé

CENTRO
ROMÁNTICO

21

12

20

C de Larramendi

C de Moraza

16

Cuesta de Aldapeta

Parque
Basoerdi

Amara
Train Station
(ET/FV)

C de
Egana

C de
Mundaiz

Bus Station
(300m)

5

Sights

Playa de Ondarreta   BEACH

1 ◉ Map p92, B3

Playa de Ondarreta, the western extension of the renowned Playa de la Concha, has a less glam, more genteel atmosphere. It's long been popular with the city's most wealthy visitors and residents (look for the former royal summer palace of Miramar that overlooks the beach). Blue-and-white-striped canvas beach 'huts' and volleyball nets dot the sands.

Parque de Alderdi de Eider   PARK

2 ◉ Map p92, F2

One of the most attractive and enjoy-able parks in San Sebastián, the Parque de Alderdi de Eider is actually more of an elongated plaza shaded by trees, dotted with benches and busy with children and families enjoying the old-fashioned carousel and numerous street artists. The park offers brilliant views over Playa de la Concha.

Ayuntamiento   HISTORIC BUILDING

3 ◉ Map p92, F1

San Sebastián's city hall is an impressive configuration of belle époque towers and domed ceilings that stands proudly at the meeting point between Playa de la Concha, the Centro Romántico and the Parte Vieja. It began life as the Gran Casino in 1897, before becoming the city hall in 1947. (Parque de Alderdi de Eider)

Understand

The Queen Goes to the Beach

Back in 1845, when going to the beach required a little more decadence than just slapping on some boardies or a bikini and flopping onto the sand, Queen Isabel II, who was suffering from skin problems that required her to bathe in the sea off San Sebastián every day, had to bring a few more essentials with her than just a trashy holiday novel.

Early in the morning the young queen would appear in a horse-drawn carriage at Playa de la Concha, before getting changed in a beach hut that was then pulled down to the water by a pair of oxen. She would then regally step into the sea to bathe before returning to her mobile beach hut (think of this as the forerunner of the caravan). The rest of her court and high society aristocrats would follow her into the sea.

It was partially thanks to this spectacle that the fashion of going to the beach for fun rather than fishing was born. Although, of course, it took more than a century before queens and princesses could go to the beach in a bikini.

GAIZKA PORTILLO BENITO/GETTY IMAGES ©

Ayuntamiento

Catedral del Buen Pastor de San Sebastián
CATHEDRAL

4 ⊙ Map p92, G3

The dominant building of the new town is the city cathedral, proudly overlooking a busy plaza. The cathedral was consecrated in 1897 and has a 75m-high bell tower. Under the foundation stone of the cathedral is a lead box containing pictures of the Spanish royal family and the pope at the time of construction. (Urdaneta 12)

Plaza de Gipuzkoa
PARK

5 ⊙ Map p92, G1

It might be called a plaza, but with its duck ponds, flower beds and many trees this square is as much a formal garden park as a city plaza. It was designed by French landscape gardner Pierre Ducasse and includes a large multicoloured flower clock. Around Christmas time a giant nativity scene fills the square.

Hotel Maria Cristina
HISTORIC BUILDING

6 ⊙ Map p92, H1

A wonderful example of belle époque architecture, the Hotel Maria Cristina was designed by Charles Mewes, the architect responsible for the Ritz hotels in Paris and London. It first opened its doors in 1912; the first guest was the regent of Spain, Maria

Understand

The Rise of San Sebastián

It was a queen with bad skin who first put San Sebastián on the international tourist map. In 1845, Queen Isabel II, who suffered from a skin allergy, was advised by her doctor to start bathing in the waters of the southern Bay of Biscay, which have long been known for their therapeutic properties. Her presence each summer attracted the rest of the royal court as well as plenty of aristocrats.

Belle Époque Expansion

The town's increasing popularity brought wealth and development. In 1864 the old city walls were demolished and the new city (Centro Romántico) came into being. During the early part of the 20th century, San Sebastián reached the pinnacle of its fame when Queen Maria Cristina and her court spent the summers here in the Palacio Miramar. It was during this period that the city was given its superb belle époque makeover that has left it with a legacy of elegant art nouveau buildings and beachfront swagger. Even World War I couldn't put a damper on the party, when the city was used by the European elite as a retreat from the war raging elsewhere.

Re-Emergence

But the good times didn't last. The combined effects of the Spanish Civil War followed by World War II finally put out the lights, and for decades the city languished. It's only in recent years that the tide has again turned in San Sebastián's favour. In the latter half of the 20th century, the city underwent a major revival. Its overall style and excitement are giving it a growing reputation as an important venue for international cultural and commercial events. The beachfront area now contains some of the most expensive properties in Spain and the city is firmly entrenched on the Spanish tourist trail, which gives it a highly international feel.

Its most recent accolade was its designation as a European Capital of Culture, a title it shares with the Polish city of Wrocław (2016).

Cristina. Today, anyone can enter the lobby and admire the understated luxury, or browse the items on sale at the San Sebastián Food Gourmet Shop (p101). (📞943 43 76 00; www.starwoodhotels.com; Paseo de la República Argentina 4)

San Sebastián Food
TOUR, COOKING COURSE

 7 ◉ Map p92, H1

The highly recommended San Sebastián Food runs an array of *pintxo* tasting tours (from €95) and cookery courses (from €145) in and around the city, as well as wine tastings (from €45). The shop/booking office also sells an array of high-quality local food and drink products. (📞943 42 11 43; www.sansebastianfood.com; Hotel Maria Cristina, Paseo de la República Argentina 4)

Puente de Maria Cristina
BRIDGE

8 ◉ Map p92, H3

Several bridges span the narrow Río Urumea, but by far the most impressive is the Puente de Maria Cristina. The belle époque creation is most notable for the angels that guard the entrance to each side. (Paseo de Arból de Guernica)

Jardines de Miramar
PARK

9 ◉ Map p92, B4

Overlooking Playa de la Concha and Playa de Ondarreta, the grassy lawns of the Jardines de Miramar slope gently down to the ocean and are a popular place to catch some sun

Top Tip

Peine del Viento

A symbol of the city, the Peine del Viento (wind comb) sculpture, which sits below Monte Igueldo at the far western end of the Bahía de la Concha, is the work of well-known Basque sculptor Eduardo Chillida and architect Luis Peña Ganchegui. It makes for a great hour-long walk from the new town. On stormy days, waves crash between the rocks and add to the drama.

with those who don't like to get sand between their toes.

Palacio Miramar
PALACE

10 ◉ Map p92, C4

When a royal family comes to the seaside, they need a suitable summer beach pad. For Maria Cristina and family, that beach pad was the Palacio Miramar. It was built in the late 19th century in a 'Queen Anne English Cottage' style (some cottage!) but sadly the interior isn't often open to the public. (Paseo de la Concha)

Eating

Antonio Bar
PINTXOS €

 11 ✕ Map p92, H2

One of the best *pintxos* bars in the new city, Antonio Bar packs them in for house specials like prawn ravioli;

the peppers are also worth fawning over. It's a small place that from the outside looks more like the sort of cafe you'd get in a train station waiting room. (www.antoniobar.com; Calle de Vergara 3; pintxos from €2.50)

Casa Valles

PINTXOS €€

12 Map p92, G3

Well away from the tourist hustle and bustle is this locals' institution that serves some of the new town's best *pintxos* beneath a forest of hung hams. The best of the lot is the *tortilla de bacalao* (salted cod tortilla). It also does *raciones* (large tapas servings) and full meals. (Calle de los Reyes Católicos 10; pintxos €2.50-3, mains €15-25; ◷1-3pm & 8.30-11pm)

Rojo y Negro

PINTXOS €

13 Map p92, F3

You can eat a full sit-down meal at this locals' bar, but we'd suggest that you come just for the *pintxos*. House specials include squid cooked on a

Local Life

Riverside Walks

The Río Urumea runs through the middle of San Sebastián, separating the new town from the Gros neighbourhood. The river is largely overlooked by visitors, but locals love to stroll the walkways that run along the banks, scattered with small areas of parkland and children's playgrounds.

plancha (hot plate) and the mushroom and prawn kebab. For breakfast try the *tosta Catalan*: toast, tomato, olive oil and garlic. (www.barrojoynegro.es; Calle San Marcial 52; pintxos from €2; ◷7am-1am)

Lanziego

BASQUE €€€

14 Map p92, F3

Just back from Playa de la Concha, Lanziego is all smart elegance and traditional white-linen dining. Although the food might lack some of the pop-art cool of the better-known San Sebastián eateries, everything here is about old-fashioned quality Basque cuisine with the seafood being a real standout. (☎943 46 23 84; www.lanziego. com; Calle del Triunfo 3; menús from €49, mains €19-26; ◷1-3pm & 8-11pm Tue-Sun)

Kata 4

SEAFOOD €€

15 Map p92, H2

An urbane crowd gather at this fashionable spot near the Hotel Maria Cristina to feast on fresh-off-the-boat oysters, delicious tuna and fruit *pintxos*, and refined seafood dishes. As well as *pintxos*, there's a daily fixed-price menu and a restaurant à la carte selection. (☎943 42 72 28; www.kata4.com; Santa Catalina Plaza 4; pintxos from €2.50, mains €14-20; ◷8am-11pm Mon-Thu, to 2.30am Fri, 10am-2.30am Sat, 11am-4pm Sun)

La Madame

FUSION €€

16 Map p92, F4

For a break from *pintxos* and classic Basque cooking, search out this

Pintxos (tapas)

modern New York–style set-up a block back from the beach. A restaurant cum lounge bar, it specialises in innovative fusion fare – think Moroccan-spiced lamb or hake with Thai coconut broth – and creative cocktails. Brunch is served at the weekend and regular DJ sets ensure an atmosphere. (☎943 44 42 69; www.lamadamesansebastian.com; Calle San Bortolomé 35; mains €14-20; ⊙6pm-late Mon & Wed-Fri, noon-5pm & 8pm-late Sat & Sun)

Drinking

Museo del Whisky   BAR

17 Map p92, G1

Appropriately named, this piano bar is full of bottles of Scotland's finest

(3400 bottles to be exact) as well as a museum's worth of whisky-related knick-knacks – old bottles, tacky mugs and glasses, and a nice, dusty atmosphere. (www.museodelwhisky.com; Alameda Boulevard 5; ⊙3.30pm-3.30am)

Koh Tao   CAFE

18 Map p92, G1

A great, friendly cafe on the edge of the Parte Vieja. Good at any time of the day, it's a laid-back place with mismatched vintage furniture, comfy armchairs and cool tunes – the ideal spot to check your email over a coffee or kick back with an early evening drink. (Calle Bengoechea 2; ⊙7.30am-10pm Mon-Fri, 9am-2am Sat & Sun)

Botanika

CAFE

19 🚇 Map p92, H3

Escape the beachfront hordes at this gem of a cafe. Housed in a river-facing residential block, it's popular with locals of all ages who flock to the small, leafy patio and sunny, art-filled interior to chat over wine and snack on salads and falafel. It also stages occasional live jazz. (Paseo de Arból de Guernica 8; ⏰9am-11pm Mon-Thu, to midnight Fri & Sat, 10am-10pm Sun)

Pub Drop

PUB

20 🚇 Map p92, H4

One of a number of haunts on a popular drinking strip near the cathedral, this shabby-hip bar is the place to get to grips with the local beer. There are up to 50 craft ales on offer, including several strong, hoppy brews from the aptly named Basque Brewing project. (Reyes Católicos 18; ⏰3pm-midnight Mon-Wed, 11am-midnight Thu & Sun, to 4am Fri & Sat)

Top Tip

Art Nouveau Tours

The tourist office gives out a magazine-style city guide that includes short walking tours that take in the new town's most impressive belle époque buildings. Guided tours are also available.

Splash

BAR

21 🚇 Map p92, G3

A bright, modern bar with outdoor seating and pop beats inside. (Sánchez Toca 1; ⏰10am-late)

Bataplan Disco

CLUB

22 🚇 Map p92, E3

San Sebastián's top club, a classic disco housed in a grand seafront complex, sets the stage for memorable beachside partying. The club action kicks in late, but in summer you can warm up with a drink or two on the street-level terrace. Note that door selection can be arbitrary and groups of men might have trouble getting in. (📞943 47 36 01; www.bataplandisco.com; Paseo de la Concha; ⏰club midnight-7am Thu-Sat, terrace 2pm-2.30am Jun-Sep)

Entertainment

Teatro Victoria Eugenia

THEATRE

23 ⭐ Map p92, G1

For over a hundred years the city's belle époque theatre has entertained the people of San Sebastián with a varied collection of theatre and classical music. It's also the main stage for the prestigious San Sebastián Film Festival. (📞943 48 11 60; www.victoriaeugenia.com; Paseo de la República Argentina 2; tickets from €19)

Shopping

In addition to the big chains, there are loads of chic boutiques selling clothing from independent designers.

San Sebastián Food Gourmet Shop FOOD & DRINK

Located inside the lobby of the chic Hotel Maria Cristina (see 6 ⊙ Map p92, H1), this is where those with a real appreciation of fine food and wine come to do their shopping. It also offers customised hampers and international shipping, as well as a wide selection of edible souvenirs, tableware and gourmet gifts. Check out its foodie tours (p133) and cooking classes as well. (www.shop.sansebastian food.com; Hotel Maria Cristina, Republica Argentina 4; ⊙9.30am-8pm Mon-Fri, 10am-7pm Sat & Sun)

Follow Me San Sebastián FOOD & DRINK

24 Map p92, F3

A small selection of top-quality regional wine and foodstuffs. You can also learn all about their products on one of the gastronomic tours. (www.justfollowme.com; Calle de Zubieta 7; ⊙10am-2pm & 4-8pm Mon-Sat)

Chocolates de Mendaro FOOD

25 🔒 Map p92, H2

We dare you to walk past this fabulous old chocolate shop and resist the temptation to step inside. (www.chocolatesdemendaro.com; Calle de Echaide 6; ⊙10am-2pm & 4-8pm)

Loreak Mendian CLOTHING

26 🔒 Map p92, G2

The San Sebastián branch of Basque brand Loreak Mendian specialises in affordable fashions for men and women, selling everything from T-shirts and hoodies to dresses and lightweight sweaters. (www.loreakmendian.com; Calle de Hernani 27; ⊙10.30am-8pm Mon-Sat)

Benegas BEAUTY

27 🔒 Map p92, G1

A historic perfume shop stocking leading international brands and in-house creations such as the herby, fruit-scented Benegas cologne. You'll also find make-up and gents' grooming products. (Calle de Garibay 12; ⊙10am-1.15pm & 4-8pm Mon-Sat)

Explore

San Sebastián Gros

The beachside neighbourhood of Gros is cool, young and pure surf fashion. The neighbourhood largely lacks the architectural pleasures of other parts of the city, but with a long surfboard-cluttered beach, some of the best-value hotels in the city and a reputation as a *pintxo* powerhouse, you're likely to spend a lot of time having fun here.

The Sights in a Day

Gros is all about the beach, but as you're waiting for the day to heat up, go for a morning stroll around the **Parque de Cristina Enea** (p105). You could even take a picnic breakfast and eat it on the wide lawns while pompous peacocks strut past. Next, head over to **Pukas** (p105) for a pre-lunch surf lesson. You'll be thrown about, but the experience will build up an appetite.

For lunch, check out the impressive **Kursaal** (p105) building where you'll find the equally impressive **Restaurante Ni Neu** (p108). After a morning of hectic activity and stomach-pleasing delight you'll need a little nap. Join the cool kids down on the sands of **Playa de Gros** (pictured; p105) and watch the experienced surfers show you how its done.

As the day cools off, head to Sagües and **Monte Ulia** (p105) at the eastern end of the beach for what might be the best sunset in town. For dinner give the *pintxos* bars of the Parte Vieja a miss and instead check out the creative culinary scene in Gros.

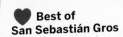

Best of San Sebastián Gros

Eating
Bergara Bar (p107)

Architecture
Kursaal (p105)

For Kids
Parque de Cristina Enea (p105)

Beaches
Playa de Gros (p105)

Getting There

Foot Gros is just over the Puente de Zurriola (Zurriola Bridge), which leads to the Parte Vieja and the new town. There's no need to use public transport to get here.

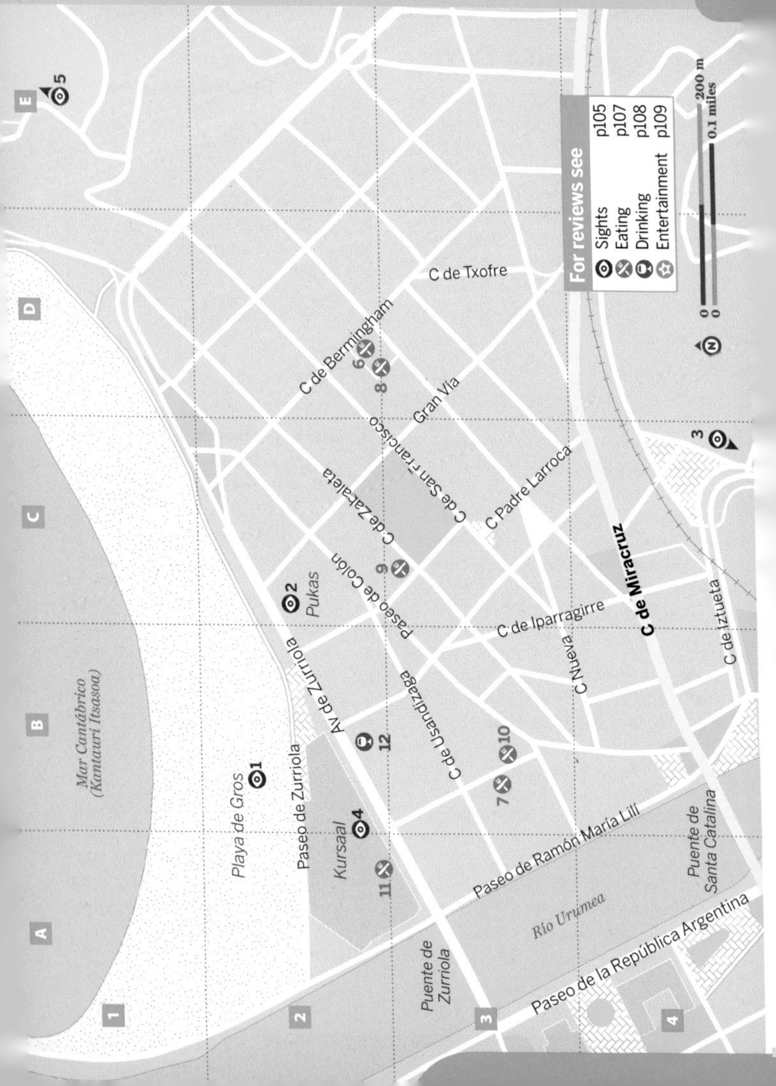

200 m
0.1 miles

Ⓔ ⊙5

Ⓓ

C de Txofre

C de Bermingham

⊗6
8⊗

Gran Via

C de San Francisco

C de Zalaieta

C Padre Larroca

Ⓒ

⊗9

Paseo de Colón

C de Iparragirre

C de Miracruz

C de Iztueta

Mar Cantábrico
(Kantauri Itsasoa)

⊙2
Pukas

⊙1
Playa de Gros

Paseo de Zurriola

Av de Zurriola

C de Usandizaga

C Nueva

Ⓑ

℗12

⊗10
7⊗

⊙4

Kursaal

11⊗

Paseo de Ramón María Lili

Puente de
Santa Catalina

Río Urumea

⊙3

Puente de
Zurriola

Paseo de la República Argentina

Sights

Playa de Gros
BEACH

1 ⊙ Map p104, B2

Less popular than nearby Playa de la Concha, but just as showy, Playa de Gros (also known as Playa de la Zurriola)is the city's main surf beach. Though swimming here is more dangerous, it has more of a local vibe. It's located east of the Río Urumea.

Pukas
SURFING

2 ⊙ Map p104, C2

Playa de Gros, with its generally mellow and easy waves, is a good place for learners to come to grips with surfing. Aspiring surfers should drop by Pukas, where lessons and board and wetsuit hire are available. Prices vary depending on group size and lesson length, but start at €64 for a weekend course comprising a 1½-hour lesson each day. (☑943 32 00 68; www.pukassurf.com; Paseo de Zurriola 24)

Parque de Cristina Enea
PARK

3 ⊙ Map p104, C4

Created by the Duke of Mandas in honour of his wife, the Parque de Cristina Enea is a favourite escape for locals. This formal park, the most attractive in the city, contains ornamental plants, ducks and peacocks, and open lawns. (Paseo Duque de Manda)

Local Life
Sagüés Sunsets

San Sebastián's location ensures it has endless places from which to admire the setting summer sun, but for the best sunset of all head to the Sagüés neighbourhood at the far eastern end of Playa de Gros. Up high on Monte Ulia is also another top sunset spot.

Kursaal
BUILDING

4 ⊙ Map p104, B2

Designed by Rafael Moneo, the Kursaal is one of the city's most beloved and noteworthy buildings. Consisting of two cubes made of translucent glass, the structure, which serves as San Sebastián's cultural and conference centre, was designed to represent two beached rocks. A lively array of musical and cultural events are held here year-round. (☑943 00 30 00; www.kursaal.eus; Zurriola Hiribidea 1)

Monte Ulia
VIEWPOINT

5 ⊙ Map p104, E1

Monte Ulia is just moments from the city centre, but in terms of peace and tranquillity it's worlds away. To get here, follow the road just behind the houses and bars at the far eastern end of Playa de Gros up to the cliffs. You can walk from here all the way to Pasajes.

Understand

Cider

For the Basques, cider came before wine. The cool, rain-soaked hills of the Basque Country are ideal for growing apples and, like elsewhere, where you find apples, you can bet you'll find cider as well. Basque cider is generally considered 'natural', in that it's not sparkling like most other European ciders. In order to add a little fizz, the cider is poured from wooden barrels into the glass from about arm's height.

A *sagardotegi* (*sidrería* in Spanish) is a cider house. They're one of the great institutions of Basque life and are particularly popular with groups of friends (people generally don't go to a *sagardotegi* alone). A *sagardotegi* isn't just about drinking cider, however, as they also serve food. Traditionally, a meal starts with a cod omelette, before moving on to charcoal-grilled steaks the size of a cow and finishing with dessert, which is invariably the local Idiazabal cheese with walnuts.

A night in a *sagardotegi* can be great fun. The average cost of a meal is around €25 to €30 per person, which includes all the cider you can drink. But you don't just go and get more cider as and when you please. Tradition states that each group of diners has someone who calls out '*txotx*' at regular intervals. This is your cue to get up from the table and head to the big barrels where either a bar man or the leader of your group opens the tap and everyone takes turns filling up before heading back to the table and awaiting the next round.

It's possible to visit a number of cider orchards and manufacturers, though keep in mind that cider season is mid-January to late May and many cider houses are only open during this period. One place that's close to San Sebastián is **Ola Sagardotegia** (☎943 62 31 30; www.olasa-gardotegia.net; Meaka auzoa 102, Irún; adult/child €8/3; ☺1-8pm Tue-Fri), near the town of Irun, which offers half-hour tours of the cider production process and includes a tasting. Visits are by reservation only. There's also **Sagardoetxea** (☎943 55 05 75; www.sagardoetxea.com; Kale Nagusia 48, Astigarraga; adult/child €4/free; ☺11am-1.30pm & 4-7.30pm Jul & Aug, 11am-1.30pm & 4-7.30pm Tue-Sat, 11am-1.30pm Sun Sep-Jun), a cider museum, where you can tour an orchard, taste a tipple of cider and learn all you ever wanted to know about the drink. It's located on the edge of the little town of Astigarraga, a short way south of San Sebastián.

Eating

Bergara Bar
PINTXOS €€

 6 Map p104, D2

The Bergara Bar is one of the most highly regarded *pintxo* bars in Gros and has a mouth-watering array of delights piled onto the bar counter, as well as others chalked up onto the board. (www.pinchosbergara.es; General Artetxe 8; pintxos from €2.50; ⏰9am-11pm)

Ramuntxo Berri
BASQUE €

 7 Map p104, B3

Anyone else smell a bargain? The well-prepared dishes served here, which are largely traditional Basque, would cost double the price if this restaurant were located in the old town. It's so popular with locals at lunchtime you might have to queue for a table. (Calle Peña y Goñi 10; mains €10-14, menú del día €11.50; ⏰9am-4.30pm & 7pm-midnight Mon-Sat, 9am-5pm Sun)

Pagadi Taberna
PINTXOS €

 8 Map p104, D2

This is a solidly locals' bar offering a big array of traditional *pintxos*, most of which are consumed by old guys who look like they've been propping up the bar since they were in their teens. The tortilla gets high marks. (www.pagaditaberna.es; General Arteche 1; pintxos from €1.80)

Bar Diz
PINTXOS €

 9 Map p104, C3

This tiny bar in beach-blessed Gros has massively good *pintxos*; other foreign tourists are rare so it's a totally local affair. If you're hungry, opt for a *ración* (plate). The breakfast isn't bad either. (Calle Zabaleta 17; pintxos from €2.50; ⏰8am-late)

Understand
Camino del Norte
- - - - - - - -

For more than 1000 years, Christian pilgrims have been walking the Camino de Santiago to reach the tomb of St James in Santiago de Compostela. The main route, known as the Camino de Francés, lies some way to the south, but an alternative path follows the northern seaboard. Recently designated a Unesco-listed trail, the Camino del Norte, or Ruta de la Costa (Coastal Route), snakes its way from Irún on the French border through the Basque Country, Cantabria and Asturia to Santiago. It's a tough 825km hike that involves plenty of arduous mountain work but rewards with some wonderful scenery. For a taste, the first leg runs from Irún to Hondarribia and on to Pasajes and San Sebastián, entering town via Playa de Gros.

Bodega Donostiarra   PINTXOS €

10 🍴 Map p104, B3

The stone walls, potted plants and window ornaments give this place a real old-fashioned French bistro look, but at the same time it feels very up to date and modern. Although initial impressions make you think the food would be very snooty, it's actually best known for humble *jamón*, chorizo and, most of all, tortilla. (www.bodegadonostiarra.com; Calle de Peña y Goñi 13; pintxos from €2.50, mains €9; ⏱9.30am-midnight Mon-Sat)

Restaurante Ni Neu   CONTEMPORARY BASQUE €€€

11 🍴 Map p104, A2

The light, fluffy and utterly modern dishes of the Restaurante Ni Neu will leave you never wanting to eat old-fashioned meat and two veg again. Throw in a spectacular setting inside the Kursaal (p105), with a view straight over Playa de Gros and bargain-priced meals, and you get a place that's hard to beat. (📞943 00 31 62; www.restaurantenineu.com; Avenida de Zurriola 1; menús €18-38; ⏱1-3.30pm Tue, Wed & Sun, 1-3.30pm & 8.30-10.30pm Thu-Sat)

NITO/SHUTTERSTOCK ©

Kursaal

Understand
Surfing in & Around San Sebastián

The opportunity to get into the waves is a major attraction for beginners and experts alike travelling along the Basque coast. The variety of surf spots along this coast is impressive and ranges from gentle beach breaks, scary slab reefs and, of course, the barrelling rivermouth lefts of Mundaka (p67). On a good day, there's no doubt that Mundaka is one of the best waves in the world. However, it's not very consistent, and when it's on, it's always very busy and ugly. Zarautz (p69) is the next big Basque surf spot. It's best on smaller swells and is a good place for beginners to take to the waters.

There are several good spots close to Bilbao with the best known being Sopelana. In San Sebastián, Playa de Gros (p105) is a good place to learn. Many of the region's better waves, though, are fiercely guarded secrets. Despite the flow of vans loaded down with boards passing along the Basque coast in summer, the prime surf season is autumn through spring.

Drinking

Bar Ondarra   BAR

12 🍷 Map p104, B2

Head over to Gros for this terrific bar, which is just across the road from the beach. There's a great chilled-out mixed crowd, and every kind of sound gets aired in the rockin' downstairs area. (Avenida de Zurriola 16)

Entertainment

Kursaal   LIVE PERFORMANCE

An energetic and exciting array of performances are staged inside the arresting Kursaal centre (see 4 ◎ Map p104, B2). These can vary from classical music concerts to dance and rock shows. Check out the website for listings of upcoming events. (📞943 00 30 00; www.kursaal.eus; Zurriola Hiribidea 1)

Explore

Hondarribia & Pasajes

With its walled *casco histórico* (historic centre), buzzing beach scene and fabulous eateries, Hondarribia makes for a wonderful day trip. The town, 20km from San Sebastián on the French border, lies to the east of Pasajes, a historic port with a charming inner core. Interest here is focused on the fascinating whaling museum and the many excellent seafood restaurants.

The Sights in a Day

☀️ Pasajes and Hondarribia in a day is a big ask without your own wheels, but it's not impossible. Start in Pasajes San Pedro, where you can visit the wonderful **Albaola Foundation** (p113) and see a 16th-century whaling galleon being built. Next, take the boat over to San Juan to visit the **Casa Museo Victor Hugo** (p113) and enjoy a slap-up seafood lunch at **Casa Cámara** (p115).

☀️ After lunch, push on to Hondarribia – ideally by car or taxi (approximately €25 to €30). Otherwise, you'll have to take bus E20 from Escalerillas, a road that's about 15 minutes' walk from San Pedro. In Hondarribia, check out the **Casco Histórico** (p113), home to the **Castillo de Carlos V** (p114) and **Iglesia de Santa María de la Asunción** (p114), and lap up the vibe on the seafront promenade.

🌙 Dine at trend-setting **Arroka Berri** (p115) or hit one of the heaving *pintxos* bars on **Calle San Pedro** (p114), Hondarribia's most lively and picturesque street.

💜 **Best of Hondarribia & Pasajes**

Eating
La Hermandad de Pescadores (p115)

Museums
Albaola Foundation (p113)

Beaches
Playa de C(p114)

Getting There

🚌 **Bus** From San Sebastián, take bus E08 or E09 for Pasajes; bus E21 is for Hondarribia. Bus E20 connects Pasajes and Hondarribia.

⚓ **Boat** In July and August, there's a daily boat from San Sebastián to Pasajes (€12/8 per adult/child), departing at 10.15am.

🚗 **Car** Pasajes is 5km east of San Sebastián; Hondarribia is about 20km, near San Sebastián's airport.

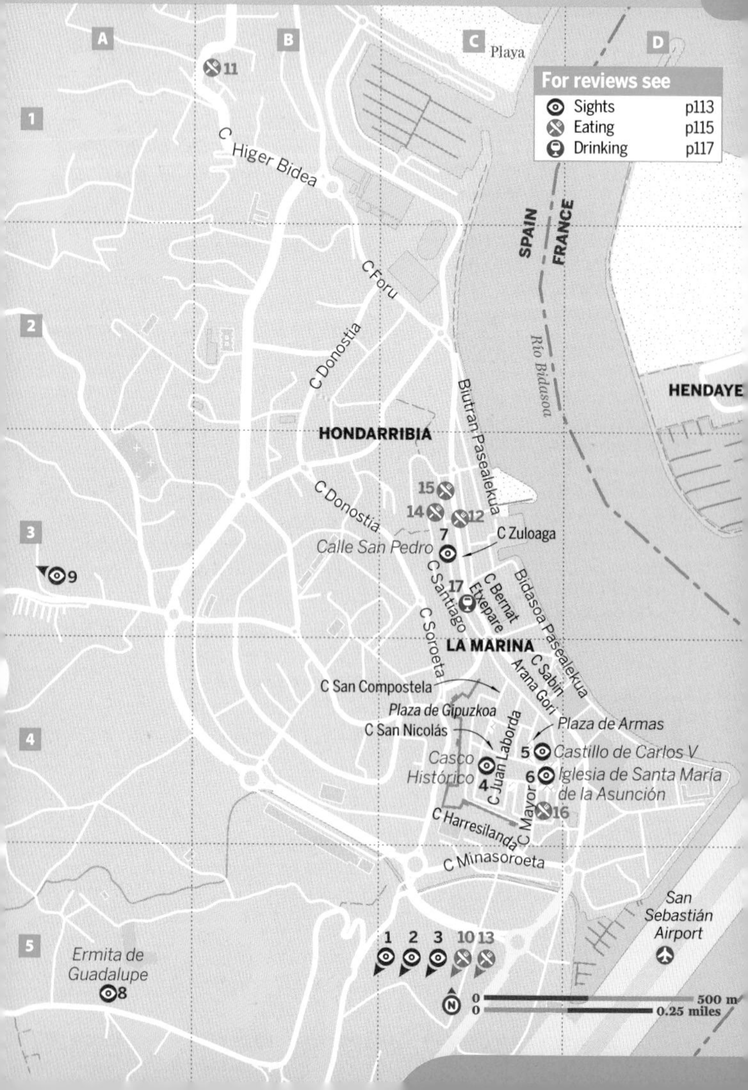

A
B
C
D
1
2
3
4
5
Playa
For reviews see
Sights p113
Eating p115
Drinking p117
11
C Higer Bidea
C Foru
SPAIN
FRANCE
Río Bidasoa
HENDAYE
C Donostia
HONDARRIBIA
Biutran Pasealekua
15
14
12
C Donostia
7
C Zuloaga
Calle San Pedro
9
C Santiago
17
C Bernat Etxepare
Bidasoa Pasealekua
C Soroeta
LA MARINA
C Sabin Arana Gori
C San Compostela
Plaza de Gipuzkoa
C San Nicolás
C Juan Laborda
Plaza de Armas
5 Castillo de Carlos V
Casco Histórico
4
6 Iglesia de Santa María de la Asunción
C Mayor
16
C Harresilanda
C Minasoroeta
San Sebastián Airport
1
2
3
10
13
Ermita de Guadalupe
8
N
0
500 m
0
0.25 miles

Sights

Albaola Foundation MUSEUM

1 Map p112, C5

This terrific museum charts the history of Pasajes' whaling industry. At the centre of the story is the *San Juan*, a galleon that sunk off the coast of Newfoundland in 1565. Models and explanatory panels describe the ship and illustrate how a team of Canadian underwater archaeologists discovered its wreck in 1978. The highlight, though, is a life-size replica of the ship that they are building, using the same techniques and materials that were used on the original. (943 39 24 26; www.albaola.com; Ondartxo Ibilbida 1, Pasajes; adult/reduced €7/5; 10am-2pm & 3-7pm Easter-Sep, to 6pm Oct-Easter)

Faro de la Plata LIGHTHOUSE

2 Map p112, C5

It's quite a climb above the town, but the views from around the lighthouse (closed to the public) are worth the effort. This is especially so when a large cargo ship slips through the cliff walls that form the entrance to the narrow but perfect port of Pasajes.

Casa Museo Victor Hugo MUSEUM

3 Map p112, C5

French author Victor Hugo spent the summer of 1843 in Pasajes, lodging at this typical waterfront house and working on his travelogue *En Voyage, Alpes et Pyrénées*. The 2nd floor retains a smattering of period furniture and various prints and first editions; the 1st floor is home to Pasajes' **tourist office**. (943 34 15 56; Calle Donibane 63, Pasajes; admission free; 9am-2pm & 4-7pm Jul & Aug, 10am-2pm & 4-6pm rest of year)

Casco Histórico AREA

4 Map p112, C4

Hondarribia's walled historic centre, much of which dates to the 15th and 16th centuries, is an atmospheric grid of graceful plazas, cobbled lanes and fetching buildings adorned with wood-carved eaves and wrought-iron balconies. The focal square is **Plaza de Armas**, where you'll find the local **tourist office** (943 64 36 77; www.hondarribia.org; Plaza de Armas 9; 9.30am-7.30pm daily Jul–mid-Sep, shorter hours rest of year), but prettier still is picture-perfect **Plaza de Gipuzkoa**.

☑ Top Tip

Pasajes Orientation

Navigating Pasajes involves learning some of the local lingo. The first thing to know is that Pasajes is more commonly referred to by its Basque name, Pasaia. Then there's the fact that the town is divided into **San Pedro** (Basque: Pasai San Pedro), where most buses arrive from San Sebastián, and **San Juan** (Basque: Pasai Donibane), over on the east shore of the estuary. A regular boat service (€0.70) connects the two districts.

Castillo de Carlos V
CASTLE

5 ⊙ Map p112, C4

Today it's a government-run hotel, but for over a thousand years this castle hosted knights and kings. Its position atop the old town hill gave it a commanding view over the strategic Bidasoa estuary, which has long marked the Spain–France border. Poke your head into the reception lobby to admire the medieval decor. (Plaza de Armas 14, Hondarribia)

Iglesia de Santa María de la Asunción
CHURCH

6 ⊙ Map p112, C4

Construction of the Iglesia de Santa María de la Asunción began in the 15th century, but works weren't completed until the 18th. This has left it with something of a mismatch of styles that includes Gothic, Renaissance and baroque. Inside is an unusual picture of the Trinity with three merged heads. (Calle Mayor, Hondarribia)

Local Life
Playa de Hondarribia

Hondarribia's **beach** (Map p112, C1) is about a kilometre from the centre. Although it's not the region's best, it's lined with bars and restaurants and offers calm swimming waters. It's very popular with locals but foreign tourists are rare.

Calle San Pedro
STREET

7 ⊙ Map p112, C3

The main drag of Hondarribia's Marina district, Calle San Pedro is a quaint pedestrian-only strip flanked by typical fishermen's houses, with facades painted bright green or blue, and wooden balconies cheerfully decorated with flower boxes. Many of the buildings now house *pintxos* bars and restaurants.

Ermita de Guadalupe
CHAPEL

8 ⊙ Map p112, A5

It's a hefty hike from Hondarribia – roughly 3km uphill – but the Ermita de Guadalupe is well worth the effort it takes to reach it (you can also drive). Dating from the 16th century but possibly sitting on much older foundations, the hermitage affords stunning views. A pilgrimage takes place here on 8 September. (Guadalupe Hermitage; Carretera Comarcal, Monte Jaizkibel)

Monte Jaizkibel
MOUNTAIN

9 ⊙ Map p112, A3

Monte Jaizkibel is a giant slab of rock that acts as a defensive wall, protecting the inland towns and fields from the angry, invading ocean. A very strenuous walking trail (about 20km) and a car-taxing road wend their way up the mountain to a ruined fortress and spectacular views. From here you can walk all the way to Pasajes.

Eating

Casa Cámara

SEAFOOD €€€

10 Map p112, C5

Managed by the same family for generations, Casa Cámara is built half on stilts over the Bay of Pasajes. The bulk of the menu is seafood based and the cooking is assured and traditional. The lobsters live in a cage lowered down through a hole in the middle of the dining area straight into the sea. (☑943 52 36 99; www.casacamara.com; Calle San Juan 79, Pasajes; menús €37-78; ☺1.30-4pm & 8.30-11pm Tue-Sun)

Arroka Berri

BASQUE €€

11 Map p112, B1

Arroka Berri isn't yet well known outside of town, but we're certain that news of its fabulous cuisine will one day spread far and wide. As with many trend-setting Basque restaurants, this one takes high-quality local produce and turns old-fashioned recipes on their head with a fun, theatrical twist. Unusually, it's open every day. (☑943 64 27 12; www.arrokaberri.com; Calle Higer Bidea 6, Hondarribia; mains €15-25; ☺1-3.30pm & 8-11pm)

La Hermandad de Pescadores

SEAFOOD €€

12 Map p112, C3

Locals in the know travel from San Sebastián to eat at this historic Hondarribia restaurant. Housed in a traditional white-and-blue cottage, it

CHANGERED/GETTY IMAGES ©

Monte Jaizkibel

serves an array of seafood classics but is best known for its *sopa de pecsado* (fish soup), said by some to be the best in the area. (☑943 64 27 38; http://hermandaddepescadores.com; Calle Zuloaga 12, Hondarribia; mains €18-21; ☺1-3.30pm & 8-11pm, closed Mon & Sun evening)

Restaurante Ziaboga Jatetxea

SEAFOOD €€

13 Map p112, C5

Pasajes is full of excellent seafood restaurants, but Ziaboga Jatetxea (there's a linguistic challenge for you) is one of the best. And with a weekday lunch *menú* of just €20, it's also very good value. The crab dishes are legendary.

Understand

A Potted History

As a frontier town in a strategic location on the French border, Hondarribia (formerly known by its Spanish name, Fuenterrabía) has spent much of its history fighting off foreign forces.

Little is known about its origins, but in 1203 it was formally recognised by the Castilian king Alfonso VIII and grew to become an important port and trade hub. But when relations broke down with France in the late 15th century, the town found itself in the front line, and, in 1498, it was all but destroyed by fire.

It was subsequently reconstructed and fortified walls were built around the hilltop centre. These saved the town on numerous occasions, most famously in 1638 when 27,000 French troops unsuccessfully besieged the city for two months. This episode, which is still a source of local pride, is commemorated every 8 September in an event called the Alarde.

Economic decline set in during the 18th and 19th centuries as perpetual warfare continued to blight the city's fortunes. These eventually took a turn for the better with the onset of modern tourism and the development of new neighbourhoods in the late 1800s. The town's fishing fleet was also revived and still today fishing is an important local industry.

Some 20km to the west, the port of Pasajes has enjoyed a rather tamer past, its fortunes tied more to the sea than the convoluted power politics of the day.

Already a working port in Roman times, it became an important medieval shipping centre and, in the 16th century, was the main point of departure for fishing and whaling expeditions to Newfoundland.

The late 19th century saw the town transformed. Industry was relocated here from San Sebastián, which at the time was launching itself as an upmarket seaside resort, and the town took on the landscape of a gritty commercial port. It retained its historic core, though, and it's this, combined with its glorious seafood restaurants, that makes it such a popular day-trip destination.

(🗹 943 51 03 95; www.ziabogapasaia.com;
Calle Donibane 91, Pasajes; menús €20-50,
mains €16-21; ⊗1-4pm Tue-Thu & Sun, 1-4pm
& 8-11pm Fri & Sat)

Gran Sol
BASQUE €€

14 Map p112, C3

Gran Sol is one of Hondarribia's best-
known eateries. Creative *pintxos*, such
as pan-fried foie gras with pineapple
juice and grated pumpkin, are served
in the woody bar, while next door
equally innovative fare is dished up
in the adjoining restaurant. (🗹 943 64
70 75; www.bargransol.com; Calle San Pedro
63-5, Hondarribia; pintxos €2.20-3.90;
⊗1-3.30pm & 8.30-11pm Tue-Sun)

Ardoka
PINTXOS €

15 Map p112, C3

A modern set-up on Hondarribia's
main bar strip with black-grey decor
and a great selection of local wines
and ciders. The *pintxos* menu lists hot
and cold offerings, including grilled
scallops and flavoursome mushrooms.
(🗹 943 64 31 69; www.ardokavinoteka.com;
Calle San Pedro 30, Hondarribia; pintxos
€1.80-4; ⊗noon-3.30pm & 6-11pm Wed-Mon)

Restaurante
Sebastián
BASQUE €€

16 Map p112, C4

In a beautiful historic building in
the middle of the old quarter, the
regarded (and rather self-regarding)
Restaurante Sebastián serves perfectly
executed traditional Basque fare and

Top Tip

From San Sebastián
on Foot

An enjoyable way of getting to
Pasajes is to walk the **coastal path**
from San Sebastián. This 7.6km
hike, part of the Camino del Norte
(p107), takes about 2½ to three
hours and passes patches of forest
and unusual cliff formations, offering lovely sea views and, halfway
along, a hidden beach that tempts
when it's hot. From San Sebastián
the route starts at the eastern end
of Playa de Gros; from Pasajes it
climbs past the lighthouse on the
western side of the port.

seafood without any of the fancy,
arty touches of some other Basque
restaurants. (🗹 943 64 01 67; www.
sebastianhondarribia.com; Calle Mayor 11,
Hondarribia; mains €15-25; ⊗1-3.30pm &
8-11pm Wed-Sun, 8-11pm Tue)

Drinking

Amona Margherita
CAFE

17 Map p112, C3

This welcoming cafe-cum-bakery is a
lovely place to catch your breath over
a coffee and home-baked cake or a
freshly squeezed fruit juice. The light,
airy interior features modern boho
decor and soft jazzy tunes. (Bernat Etxepare 1B, Hondarribia; ⊗7.30am-9pm Mon-Fri,
8am-9pm Sat & Sun)

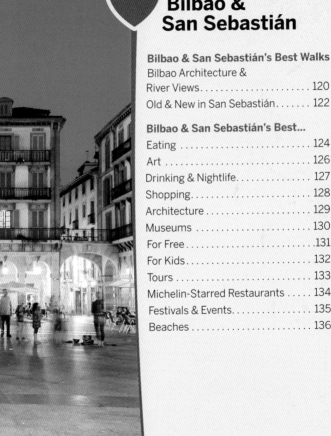

The Best of
Bilbao &
San Sebastián

Plaza de la Constitución (p79)
MATTEO COLOMBO/GETTY IMAGES ©

Best Walks
Bilbao Architecture & River Views

🏃 The Walk

Bilbao is a city that rewards those who take the time to walk its streets admiring the contrasting collections of architectural styles, enjoying the riverside walkways and sampling a drink and *pintxo* or two. This walk takes you past the most memorable buildings in the new town, crosses unusual bridges and flirts with the old city.

Start/Finish Teatro Arriaga

Length About 4km; three hours

🍴 Take a Break

You won't go hungry or thirsty while walking this route. Cafe Iruña (p50) has that perfect combination of class, history, exaggerated decoration and good drinks and food.

❶ Teatro Arriaga

Start at the neo-baroque **Teatro Arriaga** (p30) in the Casco Viejo. Built in 1890, it's home to the city opera and also hosts classical music.

❷ Plaza del Arenal

Follow the river through **Plaza del Arenal** (p33), home to children's parks and a Sunday-morning flower market. Nearby is the grand Ayuntamiento (town hall), which dates from the late 19th century.

❸ Puente Zubizuri

Continue upriver to the **Puente Zubizuri** (p46); this wave-like bridge was designed by Santiago Calatrava and is the most striking in the city.

❹ Museo Guggenheim Bilbao

Head to the most famous building in the city, the **Museo Guggenheim Bilbao** (p36) – a titanium masterpiece that changed perceptions of modern architecture.

❺ Maman & Puppy

Outside the Guggenheim check out the

NORADOA/SHUTTERSTOCK ©

Concordia train station

spider-like *Maman* and the sweetest-smelling puppy you'll ever see.

6 Iberdrola Tower

Continue walking along the river past numerous sculptures. On your left is the **Iberdrola Tower**, a 165m-high glass office block which is the tallest building in the region.

7 Parque de Doña Casilda de Iturrizar

Turn left and enjoy the stroll through the **Parque de Doña Casilda de Iturrizar** (p44) with its bandstands and duck ponds.

8 Museo de Bellas Artes

The **Museo de Bellas Artes** (p40) might not be housed inside the architectural wonder of that other Bilbao gallery, but some say the works on display often surpass those of its more famous neighbour.

9 Plaza de Federico Moyúa

The city centre is the **Plaza de Federico Moyúa** (p33). The plaza is lined by impressive buildings including the early 20th-century Flemish-style Palacio de

Chávarri and the oh-so-grand Hotel Carlton.

10 Jardines Albia

The pretty Jardines Albia, overlooked by the 16th-century **Iglesia San Vicente Mártir**, are a nice spot to rest up.

11 Concordia Train Station

At the end of Calle López de Haro is the art nouveau facade of the **Concordia train station** (p45). From here, cross the Puente del Arenal to return to your starting point.

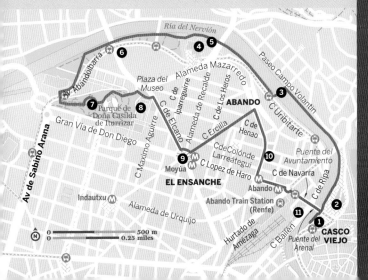

Best Walks
Old & New in San Sebastián

🏃 The Walk

Small, compact and very pedestrian-friendly, San Sebastián lends itself to gentle ambles. In the space of a few hundred metres you can pass by crowded *pintxo* bars, pretty churches, a couple of outrageously beautiful urban beaches, tempting designer clothes shops and some elegant bridges. This circular walk takes you through the best of the city centre.

Start/ Finish Parque de Alderdi de Eider

Length About 2.5km; 1½ hours

🍴 Take a Break

On this walk you can pretty much take your pick from dozens of amazing *pintxo* bars, but perhaps it's best to go for one of those in Plaza de la Constitución. Astelena (p77), with its foie-gras based treats, is our favourite here.

Ayuntamiento

❶ Parque de Alderdi de Eider

Overlooking the magnificent Playa de la Concha, the **Parque de Alderdi de Eider** (p94) is a real city social centre. It's not so much of a grassy park, but there are lots of trees and always plenty going on.

❷ Ayuntamiento

Once a casino, the **Ayuntamiento** (town hall; p94) is one of the most impressive buildings in San Sebastián, even if what goes on inside is a lot less glamorous today (but probably just as full of intrigue!).

❸ Basílica de Nuestra Señora del Coro

The intimate and artistic **Basílica de Nuestra Señora del Coro** (p79) is the Parte Vieja's best-loved church.

❹ Plaza de la Constitución

The prettiest plaza in San Sebastián, the Parte Vieja's **Plaza de la Constitución** (p79) once hosted bullfights. Today it hosts *pintxo* bars.

❺ Kursaal

Cross the river on the Puente de Zurriola (a bridge) and admire the **Kursaal** (p105) building, the city's modernist wonder. Its design is said to represent two beached rocks. Head around back to check the surf on **Playa de Gros** (p105).

❻ Hotel Maria Cristina

Cross back over the river and peek inside the lobby of the **Hotel Maria Cristina** (p95), whose first guest had royal blood. The clientele has remained similar ever since.

❼ Puente de Maria Cristina

Follow the river upstream to the prettiest bridge in the city, the **Puente de Maria Cristina** (p97). It's a belle époque creation most notable for its winged angels.

❽ Catedral del Buen Pastor de San Sebastián

From the Puente de Maria Cristina, turn right down Calle Valentín Olano, go past the fountain and over to the city's **Catedral del Buen Pastor de San Sebastián** (p95), which was consecrated in 1857. Turn right to return to the Parque de Alderdi de Eider.

Best
Eating

While in many parts of the world people eat to stay alive, in the Basque Country people live to eat. This means that dining in Bilbao, San Sebastián and around is almost certainly going to be the abiding memory of many a visit.

MARK READ/LONELY PLANET ©

Food is Life

For the average Basque, life revolves around food. Eating a sandwich at your desk is very much frowned upon here. To get the most out of the region, we'd suggest you do as the locals do and always make plenty of time for a long, leisurely lunch and a fun evening of *pintxos* (peen-chos) and drinks.

Pintxos

Enter any bar in the region and the counter is sure to be groaning under the weight of a small mountain of tiny plates of culinary art. These are *pintxos* (tapas), which will redefine your interpretation of the mere bar snack. As tempting as those lined up on the counter appear, the best are normally the hot ones made to order.

Traditional Basque Cuisine

You don't have to dine in a superstar restaurant or pick at dainty *pintxos* to have a superb meal here. Many people like nothing better than a cheap and simple meal at the local eatery. For just a few euros, you can get a lunch that in many other parts of Europe would be classed as a gourmet dining experience.

Best Pintxos

La Viña del Ensanche Go for the tasting menu at Bilbao's standout *pintxo* bar. (p47)

Bitoque de Albia Award-winning *pintxos* next to a cute Bilbao park. (p33)

La Cuchara de San Telmo Arguably the best *pintxo* bar in San Sebastián. (p77)

A Fuego Negro Dark and very cool, this San Sebastián bar has been making waves. (p76)

Bar Borda Berri Made to order *pintxos* that set the gold standard. (p77)

Bergara Bar One of the most highly regarded *pintxo* bars in San Sebastián's Gros district. (p107)

Pintxos of anchovies, tuna and red caviar

Antonio Bar Sample prawn raviolis at this small and unassuming hot spot. (p97)

Best Basque

Rio-Oja With squid floating in its own ink, pig's feet and sheep brains, this is the making of a culinary adventure you'll never forget. (p26)

Agape Restaurante A solid slice of real culinary life and a huge hit with locals. (p47)

Casa Rufo An old-fashioned spot that remains one of Bilbao's best picks for traditional Basque food. (p46)

Lanziego White-linen tablecloths just off Playa de la Concha. (p98)

Best Seafood

Karola Etxea Feast on fresh seafood in a former fishing village above Getxo's Puerto Viejo. (p60)

La Hermandad de Pescadores Diners come from miles around to try the fish soup at this Hondarribia classic. (p115)

Kata 4 Snack on sublime seafood *pintxos* and fish dishes at this fashionable San Sebastián address. (p98)

Bodegón Alejandro Casual eatery with succulent seafood delicacies. (p81)

Best
Art

PEINE DEL VIENTO SCULPTURE BY EDUARDO CHILLIDA/POLIKH/SHUTTERSTOCK ©

The Basque Country may have inspired *Guernica*, one of Picasso's most famous works, but it wasn't until the opening of the Guggenheim in 2007 that it really became a part of the international art scene. Take the time to visit some of the outstanding galleries throughout the region.

Modern Marvels

The most famous art gallery in the Basque country, and arguably in all of Spain, is the Museo Guggenheim. But the real eye candy here is the structure itself. Other galleries showcasing arresting, sometimes challenging and occasionally bizarre modern works can be found in San Sebastián.

Sober Portraits

Basque art galleries are not only focused on the bold and modern. There are galleries here with rows of dark and moody magisterial portraits of the great, good and sometimes rather unpleasant folk from days long past. Bilbao has galleries that are particularly strong in the fine arts genre.

Street Art

Great art isn't just found in the big-name art galleries of the region. In the cities look out for some impressive street art. It could be something as poignant as the copy of Picasso's *Guernica* in the town where it all happened, or it might simply be an underground graffiti artist adding his touch to the Basque Country's creative streak.

Museo Guggenheim Bilbao For many people, the Museo Guggenheim is the main reason to come to the Basque Country. Temporary exhibitions can be superb. (p36)

Museo de Bellas Artes Top collection of fine art that's often considered superior to the Guggenheim. (p40)

San Telmo Museoa Contains some impressive modern art from Basque painters and guest artists. (p72)

Peine del Viento This sculpture (pictured above) sits at the far western end of San Sebastián's Bahía de la Concha and has become a symbol of the city. (p97)

Best
Drinking &
Nightlife

The Basque Country hosts a lively drinking and nightlife scene. You can rage all night in a noisy club, jam to jazz, enjoy impressive opera or classical music and, best of all, dip a toe into the unique Basque music scene. Take note that the line dividing restaurant and bar can get rather blurred in Bilbao and San Sebastián.

EDWARD OLIVE/GETTY IMAGES ©

Teatro Arriaga Take in a classical music concert in the neo-baroque surrounds of Bilbao's beautiful old Teatro Arriaga. (p30)

Kafe Antzokia The vibrant heart of contemporary Basque culture: music, public discussions (in Basque), a cafe and beating bar. A word of caution: much Basque music is very loud. (p52)

Euskalduna Palace Enjoy classical music from Bilbao's two orchestras in this striking building. (p52)

Museo del Whisky A museum's worth of whisky and whisky paraphernalia. They claim to have over 3000 bottles of the stuff! (p99)

Altxerri Jazz Bar A temple to jazz and blues. Hosts frequent live acts from local and international musicians. (p84)

Café Iruña Ornate Moorish style and a century of gossip are the defining characteristics of this Bilbao classic. (p120)

Koh Tao Slow down over a coffee or cool drink at this friendly San Sebastián cafe. (p99)

Botanika A laid-back retreat near San Sebastián's riverfront, popular with locals of all ages. (p100)

Best
Shopping

KAROL KOZLOWSKA/SHUTTERSTOCK ©

Bilbao and San Sebastián have more than their fair share of multinational brands and out-of-town shopping malls, but in both cities, and almost every other town in the region, enough local character remains to make shopping fun. The region is particularly strong on wine and gourmet food shops. Also look out for the weekly market, a staple in virtually every town and village throughout the region.

Mercado de la Ribera
Famed as one of the largest covered markets in Spain, this is where top chefs buy their ingredients. (pictured above; p31)

Almacen Coloniales y Bacalao Gregorio Martín For 80 years this place has been selling only the finest *bacalao* (salted cod). (p31)

Arrese Divine pastries and 160 years' worth of experience to prove it. (p52)

Chocolates de Mendaro Fabulous old chocolate shop using traditional recipes that date back to 1850. (p101)

San Sebastián Food Gourmet Shop Arguably the best shop in town

to pick up a range of high-class food and wine. (p101)

Pukas Browse the latest beach wear at this San Sebastián surf specialist. (p85)

Vaho Bags made from recycled fabrics come in a blaze of colours at this hip Bilbao store. (p31)

Best
Architecture

This is an area full of startling architecture. There's the grand, the modern and the genre-changing. While a walk around any Basque city will reveal a cauldron of architectural styles, it's Bilbao that really leads the way with building mismatches. A stroll along Bilbao's riverfront and through the new town will showcase the best examples.

KAROL KOZLOWSKA/SHUTTERSTOCK ©

Best Buildings

Ayuntamiento Once a casino, San Sebastián's town hall is still beautiful. (p94)

Kursaal San Sebastián's beloved modernist work, the Kursaal cultural centre represents two beached rocks. (p105)

Museo Guggenheim Bilbao Visit at different times of the day to admire the play of light on the titanium shell. (p36)

San Telmo Museoa Blending church, garden and modern architecture into one eye-catching structure. (p72)

Azkuna Zentroa (Alhóndiga) Multi-tasking Philippe Starck creation with cinemas, a rooftop swimming pool, cafes and restaurants. (p44)

Universidad de Deusto This Bilbao landmark was designed by architect Francisco de Cubas in 1886 to house the Jesuit university. (p52)

Concordia Train Station Built in 1902, featuring a handsome art nouveau facade of wrought iron and tiles. (p45)

Best Bridges

Puente Colgante The world's first transporter bridge is still a remarkable feat of engineering. (pictured above; p58)

Puente de Maria Cristina Walk under the watchful eyes of angels on this belle époque beauty. (p97)

Best
Museums

The Basques have a particularly fascinating – and enigmatic – history and language. You can learn all about them at these regional museums which are dedicated to art and maritime history.

ANTON_IVANOV/SHUTTERSTOCK ©

Euskal Museoa The world's most complete museum of Basque history and culture. (p25)

Arkeologi Museo The Basques have lived in this neck of the woods for a long time. Find out just how long here. (p25)

Museo de la Paz de Gernika An often heart-wrenching but thought-provoking museum of war and peace. (p65)

Museo de Bellas Artes A stunning collection of religious-inspired medieval art. (p40)

Museo Marítimo Ría de Bilbao Set sail on the seven seas at this high-tech maritime museum. (p44)

San Telmo Museoa Portraying Basque culture through a wide-angled lens. (pictured above; p72)

Albaola Foundation A charming maritime museum housed in a former Pasajes boatyard. (p113)

Best
For Free

One of the delights of the Basque Country is that many of the more enjoyable sights and activities won't break the bank. In fact, they're often completely free. As well as those listed here – and all the beaches, markets, walking trails and picnic spots – remember that many museums and galleries offer free entry one day a week.

MATTEO COLOMBO/GETTY IMAGES ©

Parque de Doña Casilda de Iturrizar The most beautiful park in Bilbao is whimsical, flowery and completely free. (p44)

Monte Urgull Be king of the castle at the top of Monte Urgull and enjoy stellar views over San Sebastián. (p79)

Monte Igueldo There are plenty of reasons to spend money once you've arrived, but the bird's-eye view is still gratis. (pictured; p90)

Beaches The Basque country is home to some wonderful stretches of sand and a day on one won't cost a single euro –

unless you buy some ice cream. (p68)

Urban Ambles One of the most pleasant ways of exploring Bilbao or San Sebastián is by taking to the streets, peering into shop windows, resting on park benches and seeing where your feet take you. (p26)

Best
For Kids

ENEKO GARCIA URETA · FOTOGRAFIA/GETTY IMAGES ©

With all the outdoor activities, the Basque Country is a great place for children to have a memorable holiday. Beaches are the most obvious child-friendly day out and there are loads to choose from, but watch out for dangerous currents.

Museo Marítimo Ría de Bilbao Set sail in search of adventure (and make dad walk the plank) in this stimulating maritime museum. (p44)

Funicular de Artxanda This clanky funicular railway is a sure-fire hit with children of all ages. (p44)

Aquarium Smile at the sharks and pet the blennies in San Sebastián's homage to all that lives below the waves. (pictured; p74)

Isla de Santa Clara Row a boat out to Isla de Santa Clara off San Sebastián. (p89)

Monte Igueldo Funfair rides, ice cream and a funicular railway keeps kids happy. (p90)

Playa de Ondarreta Calm seas, volleyball nets and sandcastles on the beach. (p94)

Albaola Foundation See a 16th-century whaling ship being built at this winning Pasajes museum. (p113)

Parque de Cristina Enea This park is the most attractive in San Sebastián and a good spot to let out excess energy. (p105)

Best
Tours

Bilbao Tourist Office
(☎944 79 57 60; www.
bilbaoturismo.net; Plaza
Circular 1; ⏰9am-9pm;
@?) Organises 1½-hour
walking tours cover-
ing the old town or the
architecture in the newer
parts of town. At busy
times tours can run with
more frequency.

Bilbao Greeters (www.
bilbaogreeters.com; adult
€12) One of the more
original and interesting
ways of getting to see
the city is through the
Bilbao Greeters organisa-
tion. Essentially, a local
person takes you on a
tour, showing you their
favourite sights, places to
hang out and, of course,
pintxo bars. You need to
reserve through the web-
site at least a fortnight in
advance.

San Sebastián Food
(☎943 42 11 43; www.
sansebastianfood.com; Hotel
Maria Cristina, Paseo de
la República Argentina 4)
Highly recommended
array of *pintxo*-tasting
tours and cookery
courses – including traditional Basque cuisine
and *pintxos*-making – in
and around the city. They
also arrange wine tast-
ings. The shop/booking
office also sells an array
of high-quality local food
and drink products.

**Sabores de San Sebas-
tián** (Flavours of San
Sebastián; ☎902 44 34 42;
www.sansebastianreservas.
com; tours €18; ⏰11.30am
Tue & Thu Jul & Aug) The
tourist office runs these
two-hour tours (in Span-
ish and English; French
tours are available on

JOHN HARPER/GETTY IMAGES ©

request) of some of the
city's *pintxo* haunts.

**Follow Me San Sebas-
tián** (www.justfollowme.
com; Calle de Zubieta 7;
⏰10am-2pm & 4-8pm
Mon-Sat) Expertly run
pintxo-tasting tours of
San Sebastián as well as
cultural and hiking tours
throughout the Basque
region.

Best
Michelin-Starred
Restaurants

Boasting a cool 27 Michelin stars between them, Bilbao and San Sebastián are a mecca for gourmet travellers. The following selection of restaurants are worth planning a trip around, but make sure to book as far in advance as possible – think in terms of months, not weeks – to guarantee a table.

RAFA RIVAS/STRINGER/GETTY IMAGES ©

Mugaritz (☎943 52 24 55; www.mugaritz.com; Aldura Aldea 20, Errenteria; tasting menu €185; ☺12.30-2.30pm & 8-9.30pm, closed Sun dinner, Mon & Tue lunch) Immersed in the bucolic hills southeast of San Sebastián, Mugaritz is currently ranked the world's sixth-best restaurant. Its calling card is Chef Andoni Luis Aduriz' avant-garde cuisine and gastronomic trickery – think edible cutlery – served in a lavish 24-course tasting menu.

Arzak (☎943 27 84 65; www.arzak.info; Avenida Alcalde Jose Elosegui 273, San Sebastián; meals around €195; ☺Tue-Sat, closed Nov & late Jun) With three shining Michelin stars, acclaimed chef Juan Mari Arzak is king when it comes to *nueva cocina*

vasca (Basque nouvelle cuisine; pictured) and his restaurant is considered one of the best in the world. Arzak is now assisted by his daughter Elena, and they never cease to innovate.

Azurmendi (☎944 55 88 66; www.azurmendi.biz; Barrio Leguina, Larrabetzu; tasting menus €145-175; ☺1-3.15pm Tue-Sun & 8.30-10.15pm Fri & Sat) This celebrated three-star restaurant offers a superb setting – a contemporary steel-and-glass structure perched on a hillside 9km outside Bilbao – and innovative, cutting-edge cuisine. The Prêt à Porter bistro serves a daily €38 *menú*.

Etxanobe (☎944 42 10 71; www.etxanobe.com; Avenida Abandoibarra 4; mains €20-37, menús €75-88; ☺1-4pm

& 7.45pm-midnight Mon-Sat) Located on the 3rd floor of the Euskalduna Palace concert venue, Etxanobe is one of Bilbao's top restaurants. Its various tasting menus showcase traditional Basque dishes, as well as more modern, creative fare, while the artfully attired panoramic dining room provides a suitably refined setting.

Alameda (☎943 64 27 89; www.restaurantealameda. net; Calle Minasoroeta 1, Hondarribia; tasting menus €38-80; ☺1-3.30pm & 8-11pm, closed Sun, Mon & Tue evening) What started life as a simple tavern is now a sophisticated fine-dining restaurant, complete with garden and terrace, serving creative takes on traditional Basque cuisine, all prepared with locally sourced ingredients.

Best
Festivals & Events

The Basque love a good festival. Every town, city and most villages have their own week of mayhem and during the summer you'll almost certainly stumble upon some as you travel around. Remember, though, that for those kind of festivals you should wear red and white clothing.

Festival Internacional de Blues de Getxo
(Getxo International Blues Festival; ⊙early Jul) High-quality blues festival in Getxo, 16km north of central Bilbao.

Bilbao BBK Live
(www.bilbaobbklive.com; ⊙mid-Jul) Bilbao's biggest musical event is Bilbao BBK Live, which takes place over three days.

Jazz Euskadi
(www.jazzeuskadi.com; ⊙Jul) This is one of the region's first major jazz festivals of the summer season. It takes place over five days in the seaside suburb of Getxo.

Festividad de San Sebastián (⊙20 Jan) The city's main winter knees-up.

Regatta de Traineras (⊙Sep) Local rowers endure a marathon paddle out to sea.

Film Festival
(www.sansebastianfestival. com; ⊙Sep) The glitz and glamour of the big screen gets sandy on the beaches of San Sebastián.

Aste Nagusia (⊙Aug) Bilbao's grandest fiesta begins on the first Saturday after 15 August. The fiesta (pictured above) has a full program of cultural events over 10 days.

Best
Beaches

Life's a beach in the Basque Country and the beaches here cover the whole spectrum from tiny, rocky coves hidden down bumpy tracks to world-famous urban beauties. We've listed a few of the better-known ones, but for real fun take a slow drive along the coast allowing time to find your own favourite hidden patch of sand.

CHRISTIAN KOBER/GETTY IMAGES ©

Playa de la Concha We challenge you to find a more outrageously gorgeous and perfect city beach. (p88)

Playa de Ondarreta This is the discerning beach bum's beach. Not as showy as its neighbour, Playa de la Concha, but just as gorgeous. (p94)

Playa de Gros Where the cool kids come to play. This is San Sebastián's surf beach par excellence. (p105)

Lekeitio One of the finest beaches in Basque Country. (pictured above; p68)

Hondarribia Calm waters make this family-friendly beach a prime swimming spot for young kids. (p114)

Playa de Ereaga Getxo's sandy strip is just a metro ride away from downtown Bilbao. (p60)

Survival Guide

Survival Guide

Before You Go

When to Go

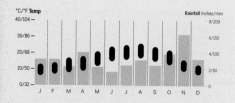

°C/°F Temp
40/104 —
30/86 —
20/68 —
10/50 —
0/32 —

Rainfall Inches/mm
8/200
6/150
4/100
2/50
0

J F M A M J J A S O N D

➡ **Spring (Mar–May)**
Unpredictable and
sometimes very wet. May
is more reliably sunny.
Tourist crowds are low.

➡ **Summer (Jun–Sep)**
Hot, waves of tourists,
endless festivals and
higher prices. June and
September are the pick
of travel months.

➡ **Autumn (Oct & Nov)**
October can be glorious,
but by November winter
is coming.

➡ **Winter (Dec–Feb)**
Wet, often cold and many
sights are closed.

Book Your Stay
☑ **Top Tip** San Sebastián
is notorious for not having
enough hotel accommoda-
tion. Book your stay for
Easter and summer up to
six months in advance.

Useful Websites
Bilbao Reservations (www.
bilbaoreservas.com) A handy
way of discovering what's
available on any given day.

Lonely Planet (www.
lonelyplanet.com) Author-
recommendation reviews
and online booking.

Tourism Euskadi (www.
tourism.euskadi.eus) The
Basque tourist board gives
loads of accommodation
suggestions.

**San Sebastián Tourist
Office** (www.sansebastian-
turismo.com) San Sebastián
gets very booked up. Let
these guys help.

Best Budget
Casual Gurea (www.
casualgurea.com; Bilbao) Arty,
modern rooms and excep-

tionally friendly staff add up to one of the best deals in the Bilbao old town.

Pensión Régil (www.pensionregil.com; San Sebastián) Proximity to Playa de la Concha makes this cute, floral choice an absolute bargain.

Best Midrange

Pensión Iturrienea Ostatua (www.iturrieneaostatua.com; Bilbao) Part farmyard, part toy shop and a total work of art, the Iturrienea Ostatua has character in abundance.

Hostal Begoña (www.hostalbegona.com; Bilbao) A stylish and individual hotel with colourful rooms and bright art. Funky bathrooms.

Pensión Aida (www.pensionesconencanto.com; San Sebastián) The owners of this excellent *pensión* (small private hotel) have read the rule book on what makes for a good hotel and have complied to the letter. The rooms are bright, bold and full of exposed stone.

Pensión Amaiur (www.pensionamaiur.com; San Sebastián) This top-notch guesthouse combines bright floral wallpaper

and Andalucian blue-and-white tiled bathrooms into a very memorable package.

Best Top End

Gran Hotel Domine (www.hoteles-silken.com; Bilbao) Designer chic all the way, this stellar hotel has views of the Guggenheim from some rooms.

Hotel Carlton (www.hotelcarlton.es; Bilbao) Class and sophistication. The rooms here have a classic old-fashioned style and the reception area is overpoweringly ornate.

Hotel Maria Cristina (www.starwoodhotels.com; San Sebastián) The hotel of choice for the actors, actresses and other Tinseltown types who pour into San Sebastián for the annual film festival.

Arriving in Bilbao & San Sebastián

☑ **Top Tip** If you've flown into Bilbao but only plan to visit San Sebastián, you can avoid going into Bilbao city centre by

taking one of the hourly buses (€15.70, 1¼ hours) direct from the airport to San Sebastián.

Bilbao Airport

➡ The airport bus (Bizkaibus A3247; €1.40, 20 minutes) departs from a stand on the extreme right as you exit the arrivals hall.

➡ The bus runs through the northwestern section of the city, passing the Museo Guggenheim, stopping at Plaza de Federico Moyúa and terminating at the Termibus (bus station).

➡ It runs from the airport every 20 minutes in summer and every 30 minutes in winter from 6.20am to midnight.

➡ Taxis from the airport to the Casco Viejo (old town) cost around €23 to €26 depending on traffic and time of day.

San Sebastián Airport

➡ San Sebastián airport is 22km out of town, near Hondarribia.

➡ It is a domestic airport and only serves Madrid, Barcelona and Palma de Mallorca.

➡ Bus E21 runs hourly to San Sebastián (€2.35, 30 minutes), stopping at Plaza de Gipuzkoa.

➡ There are regular buses between Hondarribia and San Sebastián which stop at the airport.

From the Train Stations

➡ Bilbao's Abando train station is just across the river from Plaza Arriaga and the Casco Viejo.

➡ Most accommodation is an easy walk away, but if you're lucky enough to be staying somewhere with a Guggenheim view you might consider taking the tram or a taxi.

➡ San Sebastián's train station is a 10-minute walk to the Parte Vieja; most people simply walk to their hotel or take a taxi.

Travel Passes

Creditrans give significant discounts on the Bilbao metro, tram and city bus system. They are available in €5, €10 and €15 denominations from all metro and tram stations.

From the Bus Stations

➡ Bilbao's main bus station, Termibus, is west of the centre. You can easily walk to hotels in the new town, but for elsewhere consider a taxi or the metro (the nearest station is San Mamés, a hundred metres or so away).

➡ San Sebastián's bus station is a 20-minute walk south of the Parte Vieja, between Plaza de Pio XII and the river. Local buses 26 and 28 connect the bus station with Alameda del Boulevard (€1.40, 10 minutes), which is the main road running past the Parte Vieja.

Getting Around

....

Bilbao Metro

☑ **Best for...** Moving quickly around Bilbao and its suburbs. An easy-to-understand system.

➡ Bilbao has a fast and efficient metro system that runs along two separate lines. There are stations at all the main focal points of El Ensanche and Casco Viejo.

➡ Tickets start at €1.50.

Bilbao Tram

☑ **Best for...** The easiest way to travel short distances.

➡ Bilbao's Eusko Tren tramline is a boon to locals and visitors alike. It runs between Basurtu, in the southwest of the city, and the Atxuri train station.

➡ Stops include the Termibus station, the Guggenheim, and Teatro Arriaga by the Casco Viejo.

➡ Tickets cost €1.50 and need to be validated in the machine next to the ticket dispenser before boarding.

Bus

☑ **Best for...** Public transport in San Sebastián, and for connecting the parts of the region that other forms of transport don't reach.

➡ Not many tourists use the city buses in either Bilbao or San Sebastián. However, bus 16 provides a painless way of getting from San Sebastián city centre to the base of Monte Igueldo via Playa de la Concha.

➡ Tickets cost €1.65; you can pay the driver directly.

Car

☑ **Best for...** Flexibility for out-of-town trips.

➡ If you're simply staying put in Bilbao or San Sebastián then forget about hiring a car. It will cost a lot in parking fees and you won't need it in either city.

➡ If, however, you're planning on making a number of day trips, a car is a godsend as intercity buses and trains can be irregular.

➡ There are numerous underground car parks in both cities plus metered parking (expect to pay around €12 for a full day). Parking in San Sebastián in summer can be hard work.

➡ City hotels generally charge for parking spots.

Taxi

☑ **Best for...** Convenience.

➡ As in any city, taxis are convenient and generally more expensive. Expect to pay around €10 to cross central Bilbao and a bit less to cross San Sebastián. Rates rise after dark.

Essential Information

Business Hours

The following opening hours are common throughout the region:

Banks 8.30am to 2pm Monday to Friday; some also open 4pm to 7pm Thursday and 9am to 1pm Saturday

Central Post Offices 8.30am to 9.30pm Monday to Friday, 8.30am to 2pm Saturday

Restaurants Lunch 1pm to 4pm, dinner 8pm to midnight

Shops 10am to 2pm and 4.30pm to 7.30pm or 5pm to 8pm

Discount Cards

➡ If you're in Bilbao visiting both the Guggenheim and the Museo de Bellas Artes then the combined ticket, the **Artean Pass** (adult €14), offers significant savings. It's available at both museums.

➡ The **Bilbaocard** (1/2/3-day pass €6/10/12) entitles the user to reduced rates on all city transport as well as reductions at

many sights. It can be purchased from any of the Bilbao tourist offices.

➡ The **San Sebastián Card** (3/5-day pass €8/15) entitles the user to free citywide transport, reductions at some shops and free or reduced entry to many sights. Cards are available at the tourist office.

Electricity

220V/50Hz

Emergency

Ambulance (☎061)

EU standard emergency number (☎112)

Fire Brigade (Bomberos; ☎080)

National Police (Policía Nacional; ☏091)

Bilbao Municipal Police (Policia Municipal; ☏944 20 50 00)

Money

➡ The currency in Spain is the euro (€).

➡ ATMs are widely available, but expect ATM fees on withdrawals abroad.

➡ Banks and building societies offer the best exchange rates; take your passport.

➡ Credit cards are accepted in most hotels, restaurants and shops; you may need to show your passport or other photo ID.

➡ In restaurants, you can leave small change as a tip (€1 per person); in taxis, round up to the nearest euro.

Money-Saving Tips

The days of cheap, or even free, *pintxos* (tapas) are long gone, but on Thursday evenings many bars offer some kind of deal where you pay €1 to €2 for a *pintxo* and a drink.

➡ Travellers cheques can be hard to cash; you'll probably need to go to a main branch. Commissions can be high.

Public Holidays

Many shops are closed and many attractions operate on reduced hours on the following dates:

Año Nuevo (New Year's Day) 1 January

Día de los Reyes Magos (Epiphany or Three Kings' Day) 6 January

Jueves Santo (Holy Thursday) March/April

Viernes Santo (Good Friday) March/April

Fiesta del Trabajo (Labour Day) 1 May

La Asunción (Feast of the Assumption) 15 August

Fiesta Nacional de España (Spanish National Day) 12 October

La Inmaculada Concepción (Feast of the Immaculate Conception) 8 December

Navidad (Christmas) 25 December

Safe Travel

➡ Bilbao, San Sebastián and the rest of the Basque Country is generally a very safe area to visit with few visitors experiencing any major problems. Both cities are safe to walk around at any time of the day or night. Petty theft does occur, though it's not a big problem.

➡ Car crime is a bigger problem. Cars, especially those belonging to tourists, are a particular target at beaches. Don't leave anything of value in your car.

➡ A more serious beach threat is the surf and currents. The Basque Country is serious surf country and many beaches are plagued by very dangerous undertows and large waves. Always swim in the designated swimming areas and obey lifeguards' instructions. People die every year on Basque beaches.

➡ ETA-related terrorism is, hopefully, a thing of the past, but political protests remain common and these can occasionally turn violent. If you encounter a political protest, it's best to avoid any involvement.

Telephone

Mobile Phone

➡ Local SIM cards for mobile phones are widely available and can be used in many unlocked GSM phones. Other phones may need to be set to roaming. Check with your provider if you're not sure.

➡ Data service is universal outside of some mountainous areas.

Phone Codes

International access code (☎00)

Spain country code (☎34)

Useful Numbers

International directory inquiries (☎11825)

International operator & reverse charges (collect) Europe (☎1008)

International operator Outside of Europe (☎1005)

Toilets

➡ Public toilets aren't all that common in either Bilbao or San Sebastián, though some exist around the beach area

and down by the port in San Sebastián.

➡ Many underground car parks have toilets, but they're normally only for the use of people with cars parked there.

➡ If you go into a bar or restaurant to use a toilet, it's good form to buy a drink as well.

Tourist Information

☑ **Top Tip** The Bilbao tourism authority offers an accommodation reservations department (☎902 87 72 98; www.bilbaoreservas.com), which can be very useful at busy times such as Easter. The San Sebastián tourist office keeps a list of available rooms each day.

Bilbao

Bilbao's tourist offices are well equipped and informed. Ask for the free bimonthly *Bilbao Guía*, with its entertainment

listings plus tips on restaurants, bars and nightlife.

Main Tourist Office (Map p42, G3; ☎944 79 57 60; www.bilbaoturismo.net; Plaza Circular 1; ☺9am-9pm; 📶)

Airport Tourist Office (☎944 71 03 01; www.bilbaoturismo.net; Bilbao Airport; ☺9am-9pm Mon-Sat, 9am-3pm Sun)

Guggenheim Tourist Office (Map p42, E1; www.bilbaoturismo.net; Alameda Mazarredo 66; ☺10am-7pm daily, till 3pm Sun Sep-Jun)

San Sebastián

Tourist Office (Map p78, D3; ☎943 48 11 66; www.sansebastianturismo.com; Alameda del Boulevard 8; ☺9am-8pm Mon-Sat, 10am-7pm Sun Jul-Sep, shorter hours rest of year) Offers comprehensive information on the city and Basque Country.

Dos & Don'ts

➡ **Do** greet people with the full '*Hola, buenos días*' (morning) or '*Hola, buenas tardes*' (afternoon).

➡ **Do** greet people your own age with a kiss on each cheek, although two men will only do this if close friends.

➡ **Don't** talk politics, and definitely don't talk Basque politics unless you really know your stuff.

Travellers with Disabilities

➡ Most sights in both Bilbao and San Sebastián are wheelchair accessible. However, many cheaper hotels are not. More-expensive hotels will have wheelchair-accessible rooms.

Visas

➡ Citizens or residents of EU & Schengen countries: No visa required.

➡ Citizens or residents of Australia, Canada, Israel, Japan, NZ and the USA: No visa required for tourist visits of up to 90 days.

➡ Other countries: Check with a Spanish embassy or consulate.

Language

Spanish *(español)* – often referred to as *castellano* (Castilian) to distinguish it from other languages spoken in Spain – is the most widely understood language across the country. Basque *(euskara)* is spoken in the Basque country *(el país vasco)* and is one of the four official languages of Spain. Speaking Spanish in Basque-speaking cities such as Bilbao and San Sebastián will generally be expected from a foreigner. Travellers who learn a little Spanish should be relatively well understood.

Most Spanish sounds are pronounced the same as their English counterparts. Just read our pronunciation guides as if they were English and you'll be understood. Note that 'm/f' indicates masculine and feminine forms.

To enhance your trip with a phrasebook, visit **lonelyplanet.com**. Lonely Planet iPhone phrasebooks are available through the Apple App store.

Basics

Hello.
Hola.   o·la

Goodbye.
Adiós.   a·dyos

How are you?
¿Qué tal?   ke tal

Fine, thanks.
Bien, gracias.   byen *gra*·thyas

Please.
Por favor.   por fa·*vor*

Thank you.
Gracias.   *gra*·thyas

Excuse me.
Perdón.   per·*don*

Sorry.
Lo siento.   lo syen·to

Yes./No.
Sí./No.   see/no

Do you speak (English)?
¿Habla (inglés)?   a·bla (een·*gles*)

I (don't) understand.
Yo (no) entiendo.   yo (no) en·*tyen*·do

What's your name?
¿Cómo se   *ko*·mo se
llama?   *lya*·ma

My name is ...
Me llamo ...   me *lya*·mo ...

Eating & Drinking

Can I see the menu, please?
¿Puedo ver el   pwe·do ver el
menú, por favor?   me·noo por fa·*vor*

I'm a vegetarian. (m/f)
Soy   soy
vegetariano/a.   ve·khe·ta·*rya*·no/a

Cheers!
¡Salud!   sa·*loo*

That was delicious!
¡Estaba   es·*ta*·ba
buenísimo!   bwe·*nee*·see·mo

The bill, please.
La cuenta,   la *kwen*·ta
por favor.   por fa·*vor*

I'd like ...		
Quisiera ...		kee·*sye*·ra ...
a coffee	*un café*	oon ka·*fe*
a table for two	*una mesa para dos*	oo·na me·sa pa·ra dos
a wine	*un vino*	oon vee·no
two beers	*dos cervezas*	dos ther·ve·thas

Shopping

I'd like to buy ...
Quisiera   kee·sye·ra
comprar ...   kom·prar ...

Can I look at it?
¿Puedo verlo?   pwe·do ver·lo

How much is it?
¿Cuánto cuesta?   kwan·to kwes·ta

That's very expensive.
Es muy caro.   es mooy ka·ro

Can you lower the price?
¿Podría bajar   po·dree·a ba·khar
un poco   oon po·ko
el precio?   el pre·thyo

Emergencies

Help!
¡Socorro!   so·ko·ro

Call a doctor!
¡Llame a   lya·me a oon
un médico!   me·dee·ko

Call the police!
¡Llame a   lya·me a
la policía!   la po·lee·thee·a

I'm lost. (m/f)
Estoy perdido/a.   es·toy per·dee·do/a

I'm ill. (m/f)
Estoy enfermo/a.   es·toy en·fer·mo/a

Where are the toilets?
¿Dónde están   don·de es·tan
los baños?   los ba·nyos

Time & Numbers

What time is it?
¿Qué hora es?   ke o·ra es

It's (10) o'clock.
Son (las diez).   son (las dyeth)

morning	*mañana*	ma·nya·na
afternoon	*tarde*	tar·de
evening	*noche*	no·che

yesterday	*ayer*	a·yer
today	*hoy*	oy
tomorrow	*mañana*	ma·nya·na

1	*uno*	oo·no
2	*dos*	dos
3	*tres*	tres
4	*cuatro*	kwa·tro
5	*cinco*	theen·ko
6	*seis*	seys
7	*siete*	sye·te
8	*ocho*	o·cho
9	*nueve*	nwe·ve
10	*diez*	dyeth

Transport & Directions

Where's ...?
¿Dónde está ...?   don·de es·ta ...

Where's the station?
¿Dónde está   don·de es·ta
la estación?   la es·ta·thyon

What's the address?
¿Cuál es la   kwal es la
dirección?   dee·rek·thyon

Can you show me (on the map)?
¿Me lo puede   me lo pwe·de
indicar   een·dee·kar
(en el mapa)?   (en el ma·pa)

I want to go to ...
Quisiera ir a ...   kee·sye·ra eer a ...

What time does it arrive/leave?
¿A qué hora   a ke o·ra
llega/sale?   lye·ga/sa·le

Please tell me when we get to ...
¿Puede avisarme   pwe·de a·vee·sar·me
cuando lleguemos   kwan·do lye·ge·mos
a ...?   a ...

I want to get off here.
Quiero bajarme   kye·ro ba·khar·me
aquí.   a·kee

Behind the Scenes

Send Us Your Feedback

We love to hear from travellers – your comments help make our books better. We read every word, and we guarantee that your feedback goes straight to the authors. Visit **lonelyplanet.com/contact** to submit your updates and suggestions.

Note: We may edit, reproduce and incorporate your comments in Lonely Planet products such as guidebooks, websites and digital products, so let us know if you don't want your comments reproduced or your name acknowledged. For a copy of our privacy policy visit lonelyplanet.com/privacy.

Stuart's Thanks

First and foremost I must thank my wife, Heather, and children, Jake and Grace, for their patience with this project. I know it's not easy for any of you. I would also like to thank Itziar Herrán, Oihana Lazpita, Leire Rodríguez Aramendia, Pilar Martínez de Olcoz, Clara Navas, Amaya Urberuaga and everyone else who helped.

Duncan's Thanks

Many thanks to tourist office staff Naiara Duarte, Montse Iñaki, Susana Vigiola, Ainara Lasa Larrañaga, Elizabeth Salinero, and the helpful lady at Hondarribia. Also to Lourdes Erquicia at San Sebastián Food for her brilliant tips, and, in London, to editor Lorna Parkes. As always, a big hug to Lidia and the boys, Ben and Nick.

Acknowledgments

Cover photograph: Museo Guggenheim, Bilbao, designed by Canadian-American architect Frank Gehry; Christian Kober/AWL

This Book

This 1st edition of Lonely Planet's *Pocket Bilbao & San Sebastián* was researched and written by Stuart Butler and Duncan Garwood. This guidebook was produced by the following:

Destination Editor Lorna Parkes **Product Editors** Kate Kiely, Tracy Whitmey **Senior Cartographer** Anthony Phelan **Book Designer** Mazzy Prinsep **Assisting Editors** Chris Pitts, Gabrielle Stefanos **Cover Researcher** Campbell McKenzie **Thanks to** Sasha Baskett, Carolyn Boicos, Jo Cooke, Andi Jones, Anne Mason, Karyn Noble, Martine Power, Andy Symington, Angela Tinson, Saralinda Turner, Anna Tyler, Tony Wheeler

Index

See also separate subindexes for:

Eating p150
Drinking p151
Entertainment p151
Shopping p151

Sights 000
Map Pages **000**

⊗ Eating

Our Writers

Stuart Butler

Stuart's first childhood encounters with Spain came on a school trip to Parque Nacional de Doñana in the far south of Spain and family holidays along the north coast. Early encounters left lasting impressions and when he was older he spent every summer on the Basque beaches, until one day he found he was unable to tear himself away and he's been in the region ever since. His travels for Lonely Planet, and a wide variety of magazines, have taken him beyond Spain, to the shores of the Arctic, the mountains of Asia and the savannahs of Africa. Stuart's currently writing a book about the Maasai peoples of East Africa. His website is www.stuartbutlerjournalist.com. You can also find him at lonelyplanet.com/members/stuartbutler

Duncan Garwood

Having recently spent time in Barcelona, Duncan jumped at the chance to head to the Basque Country and investigate its legendary *pintxos* bars and amazing modern architecture. A Brit travel writer based in Rome, Duncan has worked on more than 25 Lonely Planet guidebooks and foodie-related titles, including *Mediterranean Europe*, *The World's Best Street Food*, and *Food Lover's Guide to the World*. Read more about Duncan at: lonelyplanet.com/members/duncangarwood

31192020959225

Published by Lonely Planet Publications Pty Ltd
ABN 36 005 607 983
1st edition – Jan 2016
ISBN 978 1 74360 713 8
© Lonely Planet 2016   Photographs © as indicated 2016
10 9 8 7 6 5 4 3 2 1
Printed in China